## About the author

Dr Griff Foley is Associate Professor of Education and founding Director of the Centre for Popular Education at the University of Technology, Sydney, Australia. His research and publications include work on adult education theory, education and learning in social movements, informal learning, the political economy of adult education and indigenous adult education. His wide international experience has included several years teaching in Tanzania and Kenya (1968–73) as well as fieldwork in Zimbabwe in 1977 and 1982. In Australia, he developed the first training programme for Aboriginal adult educators and for several years (1986–90) directed a research project examining need and provision in Aboriginal adult education and community development in New South Wales. In 1989–91 he served as training consultant to the Commonwealth Youth Programme, South Pacific Regional Centre, in Fiji. In addition to numerous articles, contributions to books and other publications, he is the editor of *Understanding Adult Education and Training* (Allen and Unwin, Australia, 1995).

# What Scholars say about this book

A powerful and lyrical account of how engagement in social struggle can lead to learning that transforms power relations, confidence and capacity to handle change. Generous spirited, clearly written and refreshingly open, this timely book reminds us of resources for hope to set alongside global economic restructuring. *Alan Tuckett, Director, NIACE (the National Organization for Adult Learning)*

A very illuminative contribution to current conceptualizations of adult education. Professor Foley's careful reading of concrete efforts toward emancipation clearly shows how the discourse that derives from practices of resistance shapes people's understanding of political conditions and further strengthens transformative goals. His case studies of actions by disadvantaged groups to modify their reality offer strong and systematic evidence of the role of mobilization and political action as vehicles for critical learning. Readers of this book will never again take informal learning lightly. *Nelly P. Stromquist, Professor of International Development Education, University of Southern California, Los Angeles*

For adult educators who really want to assist in the struggle for democratic and radical solutions to massive social and political inequalities, there are few better places to begin their understanding than with this book. *Jane Thompson, Ruskin College, Oxford*

Global Perspectives on Adult Education and Training

Series Editors: Budd Hall with Carol Medel-Anonuevo and Griff Foley

Series Advisors: Peggy Antrobus, Phyllis Cunningham, Chris Duke, Patricia Ellis, Matthias Finger, Heribert Hinzen, Agneta Lind, Peter Mayo, Derek Mulenga, Jorge Osorio, Lalita Ramdas, Te Rippowe, Nelly P. Stromquist, Rajesh Tandon, Carlos Alberto Torres, Alan Tuckett, Shirley Walters, Makoto Yamaguchi, Karen Yarmol-Franko, Frank Youngman and Abdelwahid Yousif.

This new Series is designed to provide for the first time a genuinely global basis to the theory and practice of adult education and learning worldwide. A key goal is to introduce readers to issues, debates and understandings related to centrally important areas in adult education and training, particularly but not exclusively in the majority (or 'Third') world, and to provide a forum where practitioners from the South, women, and other social groups historically under-represented in AET, can find a voice. To this end, the new Series will contribute to redressing an imbalance in the literature whereby our understanding and debates in adult education and training in the English-speaking world have been unduly dominated by bodies of knowledge and theoretical perspectives drawn from experience in the USA and Britain and relatively unrepresentative of class, race and gender.

Among the issues of immediate and vital interest to adult educators throughout the world which new titles in this Series will address are: popular education, adult learning and civil society, post-colonial perspectives, women's perspectives, informal learning in people's struggles, worker education, environmental adult education, participatory research, the political economy of adult education, indigenous knowledge and adult learning, and the impact on them of globalization and other social trends.

## Titles already available

Shirley Walters (ed.), *Globalisation, Adult Education and Training: Impacts and Issues*

Peter Mayo, *Gramsci, Freire and Adult Education: Possibilities for Transformative Action*

Griff Foley, *Learning in Social Action: A Contribution to Understanding Informal Education*

## In preparation

Moacir Gadotti and Carlos A. Torres (eds), *Popular Education in Latin America: A Reader*

Matthias Finger and Jose Asun, *Learning Our Way Out: Adult Education at the Crossroads*

Griff Foley, Budd L. Hall, Rajesh Tandon and Michael Welton, *Adult Learning, Globalization and Civil Society*

Frank Youngman, *The Political Economy of Adult Education and Development*

For full details of this list and Zed's other subject and general catalogues, please write to: The Marketing Department, Zed Books, 7 Cynthia Street, London N1 9JF, UK

or e-mail: sales@zedbooks.demon.co.uk

Visit our website at: http://www.zedbooks.demon.co.uk

# Learning in Social Action

## A Contribution to Understanding Informal Education

*Griff Foley*

IIZ-DVV
BONN

NIACE
LEICESTER

Zed Books
LONDON • NEW YORK

*Learning in Social Action: A contribution to understanding informal education* was first published by Zed Books Ltd, 7 Cynthia Street, London N1 9JF, UK and Room 400, 175 Fifth Avenue, New York, NY 10010, USA in 1999 in association with the Institute for International Cooperation of the German Adult Education Association (IIZ-DVV), Obere Wilhelmstrasse 32, D-53225 Bonn, Germany.

Published in paperback in the United Kingdom by NIACE, the National Organization for Adult Learning, 21 De Montfort Street, Leicester LE1 7GE, UK.

Distributed exclusively in the USA by St Martin's Press, Inc., 175 Fifth Avenue, New York, NY 10010, USA.

Cover designed by Ad Lib Designs
Set in Monotype Dante by Ewan Smith
Printed and bound in Great Britain by
Biddles Ltd, Guildford and King's Lynn

A catalogue record for this book is available from the British Library

ISBN 1 85649 683 x cased
ISBN 1 85649 684 8 limp
NIACE ISBN 1 86201 067 6 limp

# Contents

# Acknowledgements

I have been carrying this book around for a long time, but in a half-conscious sort of way. Until recently, some friends and colleagues were more aware of the existence of an embryonic book than I was. I thank them for bringing it to my attention.

I wish to thank the following people who provided information and other forms of support in relation to particular case studies:

- Ian Gaillard, Carol Perry, Nan and Hugh Nicholson, Michael Murphy, Beth Hanson and Allan and Joan Davies for the Terania Creek study.
- The people associated with the two Melbourne neighbourhood houses who provided the research data and commented on the draft papers, in particular Chris Momodt, Clare Corbett, Kay McCrindle and Helen Kimberley.
- The miners who over many years have talked to me about their workplace.
- Budd Hall and Darlene Clover, for their generous hospitality in Toronto, and to Darlene for introducing me to Sonia Alvarez's work.
- The former guerrillas and *mujibas* who provided the data on learning and education in the Zimbabwe liberation struggle.

I also want to thank the many people who have read draft manuscripts of the book or encouraged me with its writing in other ways. These include Laurie and Jyoss Field, Bob Richardson, Helen White, Mike Newman, Al Thomson, Robert Molteno, Budd Hall, Bob Boughton, Peter Willis, Joyce Stalker and Peter Mayo. I am grateful to Andrew Gonczi for setting up a system of research hours which helped create time to research and write some of the material in this book. Thanks to Lucy Bantermalis for her help in completing the bibliography.

Much of the material in this book has previously appeared in journals and conference proceedings (Foley, 1991b, 1993a, 1993d, 1994,

1995a). I thank the publishers concerned for permission to reproduce the material here.

Most of all I am grateful to my wife Lori whose constant love and support have made it possible for me to write this book. Together with her mother Phyllis, her sister Margaret, her brother Ron, and the rest of their family, Lori has shown me that socialism is not an abstract ideal but is alive in the ways some working people love and help each other.

*For Lori*

. . . . . . . . . . . .

# CHAPTER I

# Introduction

This book is about some of the ways people learn, as they live, through their experiences, in their struggles. The book is also about my attempts to understand and portray the connections between learning and struggle.

> In a small Australian town in which the main industries are mining and agriculture, a family comes together for an evening. The talk is about people everyone knows. Then the conversation turns to the crisis in the coal mines. Management, wanting to severely reduce the cost of labour so Australian mines can compete with South African, Brazilian and Chinese ones, is sacking workers and attacking work practices. A miner starts talking about the inefficiency and rorts of management, which, if eliminated, would help to make mines more competitive. Before we know it we've got a list of management malpractices, from the unnecessary sub-contracting of transport to catered lunches, a list that will never appear in the mainstream mass media. A little later on in the evening one woman says to another, 'You said you wanted to learn how to make rock cakes. Come on, I'll show you'. And they bake the cakes and we eat them. Later that evening we're saying goodnight. People are getting in their cars, next to a rose bed. It's a lovely spring night and no one is in a hurry. We're looking at the roses, which are 40 years old and shooting new growth. In two minutes my brother-in-law teaches me how to prune roses, where to cut them to make the new branches go where you want them to.

I wrote this in 1987, about learning in our family, and I now think that this passage encapsulates much of what I have to say about learning. For me the most interesting and significant learning occurs informally and incidentally, in people's everyday lives. And some of the most powerful learning occurs as people struggle against oppression, as they struggle to make sense of what is happening to them and to work out ways of doing something about it.

In this book you will read of the struggles and learning of Zimbabwean guerrillas, American, Australian and Brazilian women, Australian environmentalists and workers. At the heart of the book is a notion of adult learning and education as complex and contested social activities. This conception stands against the received body of adult education theory in the English-speaking world, which focuses on individual learners, educational technique and course provision. This dominant view of adult education excludes a great deal of adult learning. Certainly the development of specific fields of adult education, such as human resource development and basic education, has ended the identification of adult education with the provision of liberal education and leisure classes. But among both adult educators and lay people, adult education is still generally equated with organised provision by professionals. Similarly, adult education research has focused largely on learning in institutionalised settings. Further, despite a recent and accelerating interest in interpretative and critical approaches to adult learning, the provision of adult education is still generally seen to be a technical and value-neutral process. (For surveys of knowledge development in adult education, see Bright, 1989; Usher and Bryant, 1989; and Peters et al., 1991).

The view of adult education as value-neutral formal provision can be – and is increasingly being – challenged on at least four grounds. First, there is clearly more to adult learning than what happens in formal courses. It is clear that the informal but systematic learning efforts of individual adults is highly significant (see Candy, 1991: 157–201 for a useful review of the literature); and in recent years the notion of organisations as learning environments has received increasing attention (see, for example, Marsick, 1987; Leymann and Kornbluth, 1989; Marsick and Watkins, 1991; Senge, 1992; Field, 1995). There is also the important informal, incidental and embedded learning which occurs in various settings – for example, in workplaces, families, communities and social movements (Foley, 1981, 1991b, 1993a, 1993c, 1993d, 1995a; Rossing, 1991). And there is an implicit informal learning dimension in accounts of the work of adult educators (see, for example, Adams, 1975; Lovett, 1975; Thompson, 1983; Newman, 1993). Secondly, adult education is not just a technical process, nor is it value-free. Like any human endeavour, adult education is a complex social and value-creating activity, one which is shaped by, and which shapes, social structure and culture, and which inevitably involves ethical judgements and choices. Thirdly, individuals and groups have different goals and interests in adult learning and education which therefore need to be understood as contested activities, that is, activities around which there is likely to be conflict. Fourthly, there is an alternative body of critical adult education scholarship, much of it from the majority world, which is informed by historical materialist theory and socialist politics. I refer to some of this work in the Conclusion to this book. The majority world contribution to this literature is usefully discussed by Hall (1993).

It follows from this argument that it is important to study adult learning in all its variety, and to identify generally unrecognised (even sometimes to those involved in them) forms and traditions of adult learning and education. This book comprises case studies of informal and incidental learning in various forms of social struggle. These case studies are located within a theoretical framework which seeks to explain connections between three sets of variables: learning and education, local politics and ideologies, and broad social forces and changes. In what follows I give an overview of the case studies, outline the theoretical framework and give the reader some sense of where I sit intellectually and politically.

## The case studies

While systematic education does occur in some social movement sites and actions, learning in such situations is largely informal and often incidental – it is tacit, embedded in action and is often not recognised as learning. The learning is therefore often potential, or only half realised. For example, when I interviewed people who had participated in a twelve-year struggle to save a remnant of rainforest in eastern Australia, they expressed surprise and delight at the learning that was revealed. It was their learning, but they had never articulated it. They had been so focused on saving the forest they had not thought about learning. Yet their learning, as we will see, was profound and is of continuing use, to themselves and others.

To more fully realise the value of such learning we need to expose it. In doing this it helps if we understand that people's everyday experience reproduces ways of thinking and acting which support the, often oppressive, status quo, but that this same experience also produces recognitions which enable people to critique and challenge the existing order. In this book you will find many examples of this complicated process of reproduction and recognition.

In Chapter 2, through an examination of case studies of women's learning in neighbourhood and workplace struggles in the United States, I argue that the unlearning of dominant, oppressive ideologies and discourses[1] and the learning of oppositional, liberatory ones are central to processes of emancipatory action. But these studies also show that processes of emancipatory learning and action are complex and contradictory.

This argument is elaborated upon in the next two chapters which are detailed studies of informal and incidental learning in two Australian situations – activists' learning in a campaign to save a rainforest, and women's learning in urban community centres. In the rainforest campaign, the subject of Chapter 3, activists experienced both instrumental and critical learning. They gained knowledge and skills in rainforest ecology, lobbying and advocacy. They also developed a more critical view of authority and expertise, and a recognition of their own ability to influence decision-making. As already noted, all this was *incidental* learning – it was embedded in the social action and not articulated until I interviewed the activists about it many years after the campaign. And this learning took place in *struggle* between the conservationists and other interest groups, and among and within the conservationists themselves.

The analysis of incidental learning in struggle is further developed in Chapter 4, which discusses the experiences of women in two Australian community centres. Struggles which took place in these centres – in the minds of individuals, among members, between workers and committee members and between the centres and the State – generated instrumental skills and knowledge, self-awareness and social and political understanding. This study also shows that such learning is not emancipatory in some linear, developmental sense, that it is complex and contradictory, shaped as it is by intra-personal, interpersonal and broader social factors.

Chapters 2–4 convey a sense of the complexity of the relationship of learning and social action at the local or community level. The analysis of this complexity is further developed in Chapters 5–7, which discuss the relationship of wider contextual and local micro-political factors in informal learning in social action. In Chapter 5, which examines education and learning in the current process of global economic restructuring, I argue that the received notion of economic 'restructuring' constitutes a myth that masks the actual processes of capitalist reorganisation. The current phase of reorganisation of the economy, workplaces and education has been misrepresented by policy-makers and many intellectuals, who are promoting simplistic technical solutions to complex social problems. To understand this restructuring and the role of education and learning in it, it is essential to understand capitalism. Capitalism is a system of economic, political and cultural domination, based on two processes: the alienation of labour (the separation of workers from the process and product of their labour), and reification (the commodification of all relationships). These relationships of domination are learned, and can be unlearned. This argument is developed through an examination of recent macro-economic change, workplace reform and educational change in Australia. Particular attention is paid to analysing how and what workers learn as they negotiate workplace change.

Chapter 5 raises a crucial issue, the relationship of capitalism to learning and action in social movements. This issue is explored further in Chapter 6, which examines the learning dimension of women's movements in Brazil during the period of military rule, capitalist economic boom and crisis, and transition to formal democracy in the period 1964 to 1989. The focus of this chapter is the relationship of economic and political change on the one hand and changes in women's political consciousness and action on the other. While broad economic and political changes created the material conditions for social movement activity, these changes did not, by themselves, generate such activity. For people to become actively involved in social movements something had to happen to their consciousness – they had to learn that social action was necessary and possible. In Brazil the oppositional discourses of human rights, social justice, feminism and liberation theology were decisive in creating the subjective conditions for political action by women.

Chapters 2–6 of the book are case studies of learning and struggle in capitalist societies. Chapter 7 examines education and learning in an avowedly anti-capitalist movement, the Zimbabwe liberation movement. Drawing on archival material and interviews, I examine the experience of resisting colonialism as a process of emancipatory learning for the colonised, and discuss the systematic education of cadres and masses in the latter phase of the liberation struggle. The central question addressed in this chapter is whether, overall, political education and learning in the Zimbabwe national struggle promoted democracy and socialism, or whether they were too weak to counter the authoritarian political culture of the settler state and the nationalist movement. In discussing this question I explore relationships between the colonial political economy, the micro-politics of the liberation movements and learning and education.

A Conclusion briefly restates the argument of the book, locates it within contemporary adult education theory, discusses some peda-gogical implications of the analysis, and suggests some directions for further research on the relationship of emancipatory struggle and learning. Through analysis of two examples, I criticise the tendency to abstract and culturalist analysis in contemporary 'radical' adult education theory. I argue for the analytical strength and political utility of holistic and materialist analyses of learning in particular sites and struggles, maintaining that a critique of capitalism must lie at the heart of emancipatory adult education theory and practice.

## Theoretical framework

The theoretical framework developed in the book has three dimensions:

1. A broad conception of education and learning.
2. An emphasis on the relationship of education and learning and collective and emancipatory struggle.
3. An analytical framework which enables connections to be made between learning and education on the one hand, and analysis of political economy, micro-politics, ideologies and discourses on the other.

*A broad conception of education and learning* The vignette about family learning which begins this book directs our attention to the need to break out of the strait-jacket which identifies adult education and learning with institutionalised provision and course-taking. Adult learning and education constitute an ensemble of activities, includ-ing, in addition to formal education: incidental learning which occurs as people live, work and engage in social action; informal education and learning in which people teach and learn from each other naturally and socially in workplaces, families, community organisations and social action; and non-formal education – structured, systematic teaching and learning, again in a range of social settings. This broader conception enables us to recognise the widespread and powerful informal and incidental education and learning that occur around social and political struggle.

*Struggle and learning*   Adult learning is a complex and diverse sphere of human activity, as central to human life as work or politics. Adult learning and education are also contextual and contested activities.

One way of understanding human history is to see it as a series of struggles between different groups. In these struggles one group – for example, feudal lords, capitalists, men, colonisers – tries to dominate another – serfs, workers, women, indigenous people. These attempts at domination usually have an economic and political basis, but they also have an ideological dimension. For example, from the fifteenth to the nineteenth centuries plantation owners in the Americas built their wealth on the work of enslaved Africans and their descendants. These planters feared the potential political power of slaves, who greatly outnumbered them. The planters devised a legal system which defined slaves as property, to be bought, sold, controlled and exploited by their 'owners'. If slaves resisted, the law provided and justified harsh punishments. A paternalistic ideology assumed that owners were responsible for the material and spiritual welfare of slaves. Paternalism both ameliorated and disguised the oppression of slaves. The ideology required owners to look after slaves; it also allowed owners to feel, and appear, virtuous.

But what owners did and believed was only one part of the story. Slaves were not passive victims. In their daily lives slaves both accommodated and resisted the demands of slave owners, and in doing so took advantage of their paternalism. Slaves' use of Christianity is a good example of this. Slaves were forced by their owners to attend church, where they were instructed in their obligations to obey their owners. But they also adopted Christianity and turned it to their own ends. They rejected the notion of racial hierarchy which was the foundation of the slave system. They asserted the side of Christianity which emphasises the equality and mutual obligation of all human beings. They held their own secret religious services, with their own black preachers. They created their own hymns, and songs that satirised the planters.[2]

In such ways slaves simultaneously accommodated to and resisted the harsh treatment and humiliation they experienced daily. Similar instances of accommodation and resistance can be found in any society. For example, in Australia and similar countries, youth who do not like school rarely run away or otherwise openly defy their teachers and parents. These adolescents accept that they have to attend school, but develop ways of undermining the authority of teachers and of creating spaces where they can have fun and avoid school work. In the longer term this resistance frequently has negative effects. For example, in a classic study conducted in the north of England in the 1960s, Paul Willis (1978) showed how working-class boys' very success in satirising and subverting the middle-class culture of their school condemned them to educational failure and low-paid menial employment.

Struggles which are more explicitly emancipatory also frequently have ambiguous and contradictory outcomes. In her history of the European women's movement, *Women, Resistance and Revolution* (1972), Sheila Rowbotham showed how, in France and England in the eighteenth and nineteenth centuries, women moved from protective and defensive resistance that left them still dependent on men, to collective consciousness and action involving popular, mobilising and creative forms of organisation and action, and a developing awareness of the complexities of social action (of, for instance, the need for both separate women's spaces, and for connections between the women's movement and the male-dominated labour movement). But Rowbotham also explored the limitations of these forms of organisation and this developing consciousness. The maintenance of patriarchal relations in the family meant that until recently many working-class women have considered work outside the home to be secondary to their domestic duties. Long periods spent in child-rearing have further served to discourage the organisation of women in workplaces, and have contributed to the social construction of women's work as poorly paid and unskilled, a definition against which women are still struggling. Moreover, this older tradition of popular, bottom-up feminism was, for most women, obscured until the appearance of 'second-wave' feminism in the 1960s (Rowbotham, 1972: 99–133).

So we can say that domination is universal, and that it is continually contested. It also makes sense to see history as a continual struggle by ordinary people to maintain and extend control over their lives. But we also need to understand that popular[3] struggles are complex, ambiguous and contradictory. This book tries to throw light on these complexities by examining the *learning dimension* of people's lives and struggles.

*The dynamics of learning in struggle*   To understand the complexities of learning in struggle we need an analytical framework which connects learning to its context. Such a framework is suggested by Sonia Alvarez (1990b) in her study of women's movements in Brazil, referred to above and the subject of Chapter 5 of this book. As already noted, this study examines the relationship of economic and political change and changes in women's political consciousness and action. Alvarez's analysis accounts for both macro-economic factors and micro-political factors. And, even though this was not her intention, Alvarez's focus on ideology and discourse provides a bridge between a rich contextualised analysis of social movement activity and an analysis of adult learning because the process of engaging with hegemonic and oppositional ideologies and discourses is a *learning* process.

Satisfactory accounts of learning in struggle make connections between learning and education on the one hand, and analysis of political economy, micro-politics, ideology and discourse (or 'discursive practices') on the other. These connections are represented in the following figure.

Political economy                                     Micro-politics

**Emancipatory
social
struggles**

Educational
interventions

Learning                 Discursive practices                 Ideologies

Exploring the relationships between these variables provides a framework for analysis of learning and social struggle in diverse situations, and suggests some key questions:

*In a particular situation:*

- What forms do education and learning take?
- What are the crucial features of the political and economic context? How do these shape education and learning?
- What are the micro-politics of the situation?
- What are the ideological and discursive practices and struggles of social movement actors and their opponents? To what extent do these practices and struggles facilitate or hinder emancipatory learning and action?
- What does all this mean for education? What interventions are possible and helpful?

In this book these questions are explored through the case studies.


## Writing the book

The research on which this book is based has been conducted over a period of twenty years. In this time my core educational and political concerns have remained constant. As indicated above, my interest is in the relationship of learning and people's struggles for a decent life. I have participated in, witnessed and researched a variety of such struggles, ranging from teachers' and students' efforts to maintain and extend control over their work, to movements for national independence. In writing about these struggles I have found it useful to attempt to link macro and micro analysis, in ways which I have outlined in the previous section and which I will elaborate upon in the rest of the book. I have also come to recognise that human action and thought are infinitely complex, ambiguous and contradictory. But this recognition has not caused me to become detached or cynical. I still believe in the decency of 'ordinary' people (those whom the American adult educator Myles Horton called so accurately 'the uncommon common people') and in their capacity to create sustainable, just and democratic societies. I also still believe that socialism and the working-class movement are central to this project. But I have come to understand that the complexities and problematic nature of popular struggles and movements must be recognised, and that only democratic means can generate emancipatory ends.

An essential part of working democratically is the development of open and transparent analyses. For this reason, I am heartened by the contemporary tendency to emphasise the socially constructed nature of research and the importance of texts drawing attention to their construction. All analyses are partial and partisan, and they must be made transparent and problematic (Ellsworth, 1989: 305, 310). In this book I will seek to do this by making my theoretical and value assumptions explicit.

I will begin by sketching my professional experience and intellectual and political position. I have worked in public education for thirty years, a quarter of that time in Africa and the rest of the time in Australia. I studied education in Uganda and taught in secondary schools in Tanzania and Kenya in the late 1960s and early 1970s. In the late 1970s and early 1980s I researched education in colonialism and liberation struggle in Zimbabwe. Since 1975 I have been involved in the professional education of adult educators in Australia.

My primary intellectual and political interest is in how people learn in emancipatory struggle. Because I look for them, I see such struggles and learning everywhere, not only where one might expect to find them, in popular movements and social action, but also in workplaces (including educational institutions) and families. I am convinced that understanding such learning is vital to the development of a truly democratic politics. I am also convinced that a genuinely emancipatory politics and economics must be socialist. What exactly I mean by 'democracy' and 'socialism' and how learning might contribute to their development will, I hope, be clearer to the reader by the end of the book.

I think it will help the reader if I say a few further things here about influences on my thinking and writing. First, as long as I can remember I have been attracted by writing that is clear in expression and strong in argument. In this I have been influenced by my father, who was a journalist and who always stressed to me the importance of succinctness. 'Never', he would tell me, 'use two words when you can use one'. Secondly, I have been greatly influenced by empirical history and sociology. The development of an argument through accumulation of data persuades me. For me, convincing theorising is inductive and dialectical, and I subscribe to Edward Thompson's dictum about the necessary dialogue of data and theory. Thirdly, historical materialism is the rock on which my analysis is built. Marxist political economy, history and cultural analysis are fundamental to my thinking. The Marxism that attracts me is reflexive and empirical. Dogmatism and excessive abstraction in Marxism or in any other problematic repel me. The Marxist writers who mean the most to me are people like Raymond Williams (1989), Sheila Rowbotham (1972, 1992), Eduardo Galeano (1989, 1992), Ellen Wood (1986, 1995), Pablo Neruda (1978) and Amilcar Cabral (1973, 1974), people whose solidarity with particular groups of people are alive in their work. Fourthly, I am interested in the ways in which people make sense of their experience and in the ways those experiences and meanings are represented. I am consequently drawn to interpretative sociology and anthropology, Marxist cultural analysis and feminist history and sociology.

I see the task of the researcher as being to write the soundest possible account of whatever is being investigated. In my own work, and in the work of scholars I admire, this has involved assembling data and subjecting them to analysis informed by solid theory. In this way I have sought the dialectic of data and theory just referred to. I have tried to allow the data to speak, which in my writing has often meant giving voice to the previously little heard – local environmental activists, suburban women, workers, the colonised. In representing learning and education as complex and contested social activities, notions of context and conflict have been central, as has the juxtaposition of micro and macro analysis. I have wanted to provide detailed accounts of the complexities and contradictions of emancipatory learning and education in particular situations.

I have recently come to realise that one of the things I have been trying to do is to construct a 'social phenomenology' of adult learning. Phenomenological research concentrates on portraying lived experience and the sense people make of it, rather than on analysing or generalising about it. As Clifford Geertz (1973: 3–30) put it, the concern is with connecting action to its sense, rather than behaviour to its determinants. And yet a powerful phenomenology will do both – it will give a rich picture of how different people in a situation make sense of it and act on it, and it will seek to make explanatory connections between this micro activity and broader cultural, political and economic processes. A phenomenology is most powerful if it is contextual, if it is *social* (McIntyre, 1996).

In writing the social phenomenologies of learning which comprise this book two things have been important to me. One has been to contextualise the learning, and in particular to show that learning and education need to be seen not, as they generally are, as technical or interpersonal processes, but as contested and infinitely complex social processes. The second thing I have tried to do is to give the reader a feeling of what the experience and learning were like for those who lived them. To again draw on Geertz (1988: 1–24), the social science accounts that convince are not the ones that overwhelm us with the weight of their data or their theoretical elegance, they are those that convey that sense of 'being there'.

In writing this book a third issue has become important for me. Different forms of writing construct social activity differently. And there can be no complete and agreed account of any social activity. These recognitions present me with a dilemma. I think that the accounts of informal learning in struggle told in this book are worth telling. But they are examples of 'universalising academic discourse'. Although these accounts make explicit their research methodology and their theoretical assumptions, each is written as 'the account', closed, final, authoritative. Hence the writing still makes it seem as if there can be a single agreed account of social reality. Understanding now how partial, constructed and unrepresentative of possible perspectives and interpretations the accounts in this book are has made me look for ways of interrupting them, undermining their tendency to objectify and 'scientise' social reality. Raising the issue of writing in this general way is one such interruption – I hope it will alert the reader to the partial and problematic nature of the accounts of learning and struggle that make up this book.

## Notes

1. In the sense used in this book, ideologies and discourses refer to the ways in which people make meaning of situations and represent them. The terms are explained in more detail at the beginning of Chapter 2.

2. The account of domination and accommodation/resistance in slavery is based on Jean Anyon's summary of Eugene Genovese's book on the plantation system in the southern states of the USA, *Roll, Jordan Roll*. See also Rodney, 1972 and Galeano, 1973, especially pp. 11–100.

3. In this book 'popular struggle' and 'emancipatory struggle' are used interchangeably. They both refer to social struggles in which people are trying to build more democratic and sustainable relationships.

# CHAPTER 2

# Ideology, Discourse and Learning

In this chapter I argue that the unlearning of dominant discourses and the learning of resistant discourses is central to emancipatory learning. I begin with a brief theoretical discussion of ideology and discourse and their relationship to learning in emancipatory struggle. I then apply these theoretical insights to three case studies of women's learning in community and workplace struggles in the United States.

## Ideology and discourse

The term 'ideology' has many meanings, the most widely known of which is 'distorted understanding', often in support of particular interests. The paternalistic ideology of the slave owners discussed in Chapter 1 of this book is an example of this use of the term. For the purposes of this book a more interesting focus is on the role of ideology in individual consciousness and social structures and relationships. Here ideology refers to the various ways in which social meanings and structures are 'produced, challenged, reproduced and transformed' in both individual consciousness and social practices and relationships. Ideology in this sense is an active process, one that is constructed (and which can be 'de-constructed' – pulled apart – and 'reconstructed' – rebuilt) by people. Ideology in this sense performs both positive and negative functions. It holds a group or society together by creating shared frameworks of meaning and values. It can also be a means of domination, of what Gramsci (1971: 12–13ff.) called 'hegemony'. In this latter sense ideology reflects, constructs and reproduces the power and interests of dominant groups in society. But hegemony is continually contested – there is continual struggle between dominant and oppositional ideologies, as for example, between the bureaucratic and environmental ideologies in the Terania Creek campaign (Chapter 3). Gramsci referred to this process of struggle between dominant and insurgent ideologies as 'hegemonic struggle'. (On these issues, see Williams, 1973; Giroux, 1984, 309–12; Kemmis and Fitzclarence, 1986: 96–8; Fairclough, 1992, 91–6.)

'Discourse' refers to examples of spoken and written language, and can be analysed as both a linguistic and a social phenomenon (Fairclough, 1992: 3ff.). For linguists, the interest is in close analysis of samples of discourse. For the sociologist the interest is in the relationship of discourse to other social practices, relationships and structures. With regard to the latter, in recent years there has been a burgeoning interest in the role of discourse in constructing and changing ideologies. The writing of the French scholar Michel Foucault has been particularly influential. Foucault's interest was in discourse as an aspect of 'soft' and 'secret' forms of domination in apparently progressive and humane modern institutions and social sciences. For Foucault, discourses are about 'what can be said and thought, but also about who can speak, when, and with what authority' (Ball, 1990: 2). Discourses are of central importance in how people understand their own identities and place in society (Fairclough, 1992: 64).

To Foucaultians, discourses are central to the production of ideology in its sense of distortion and misrepresentation, and to the construction of hegemony. As Ball points out, in dominant discourses

> the possibilities for meaning and for definition are pre-empted through the social and institutional position of those who use them. Meanings thus arise not from language but from institutional practices, from power relations. Words and concepts change their meaning and their effects as they are deployed within different discourses. Discourses constrain the possibilities of thought. They order and combine words in particular ways and exclude or displace other combinations. (Ball, 1990. Cf. Austin-Broos, 1987: 149–59; Patton, 1987: 228–33)

The notions of subject and discourse are linked to the idea of 'governance': to state it baldly, Foucault sees subjects as being governed, or controlled, by discourses. In his historical studies, Foucault traced the replacement of violent control of populations with gentler means, including the key modern social institutions like the prison, hospital, asylum, workplace and school. The discourses and practices of these institutions subtly control people (Philp, 1985: 68–78).

Foucault also speaks of 'totalising discourses', ways of thinking and acting which speak for and take over whole areas of human life. So, for example, over the past two centuries the learning dimension of human life has been colonised by the discourse of institutionalised education, and thinking about the organisation of work has come to be dominated by the discourse of management. Foucault also notes the ways in which discourses operate 'behind the backs' of their speakers. This secret, unconscious aspect of discourses means that people can participate in their own subjugation by absorbing the rules of a discourse or by taking something that is socially constructed as 'truth'. Frequently, even when people resist totalising discourses, they often do so in ways which do not challenge the power of the discourse to set the boundaries of thought (see, for example, the workers' resistance described in Chapter 5, this volume; the behaviour of the schoolboys studied by Willis (1978); and Gowen (1991), on hospital workers' resistance to management). Again, the carriers of the discourse are also generally unaware of the totalising power of what they are transmitting, and so are the unaware bearers of oppression.

These concepts drawn from Foucault construct a bleak and deterministic view of the dominative power of discourse and ideology. Yet as we will see in the studies discussed in this and subsequent chapters, dominant ideologies and discourses are continually challenged by resistant or 'insurgent' ones which people learn in struggle.

The concepts of ideology and discourse help us to understand that social reproduction and change are cultural as well as economic and political processes. Consciousness and learning are central to the processes of cultural and social reproduction and transformation. The unlearning of dominant, oppressive ideologies and discourses and the learning of insurgent, emancipatory ones are central to processes of emancipatory change. But these processes of emancipatory learning and action are not straightforward; they are complex, ambiguous, contradictory. These complexities are best understood through analysis of concrete situations – hence the focus in this book on case studies.

The feminist scholarship which burgeoned from the 1960s onwards provides a rich source of data on the development of women's political consciousness through participation in political struggle. The learning dimension of such struggles can be 'read into' many of these sociological accounts. I will review three such studies here.

## The gynaecological clinic

Sandra Morgen (1988) examined the development of working-class women's consciousness during an eight-month campaign over the closure of a gynaecological clinic in a New England city in 1977. The 'macro' context of this closure was the transformation of the social welfare state into the 'competitive state', driven by the restructuring of the US and global economies. But these broad political and economic changes were played out in a particular way in the struggle over this clinic. The decision to close the clinic was made by hospital administrators and ten white male obstetricians. The closure was opposed by a group of clinic users and workers. Tactics used successfully by the activists included surveys of users, petitions, public meetings, picketing the hospital, and lobbying bureaucrats and hospital board members. The campaign not only brought about the reopening of the clinic, it also led to the later establishment of a neighbourhood health centre.

Morgen's analysis focuses on the development of the political consciousness of the activists. Her interest is in how the activists developed an understanding of relations of power and domination through participating in the campaign. Morgen makes connections between the social conditions which created and shaped the struggle, the events of the campaign, and how the campaigners experienced and interpreted the struggle. She argues that central to the learning experienced by these activists was the development of a critique of dominant ideologies and discourses and the articulation of oppositional ideologies and discourses. This critique and articulation were developed in various media and situations. In a leaflet which the activists produced to publicise the first public meeting in the campaign, a woman is pictured brought to her knees by the burden of health-care costs, represented as little boxes on her back, labelled with the costs of doctor's fees. The leaflet calls on 'working women' to meet to discuss the closure of the clinics, and charges the hospital with 'forgetting its responsibility to the working women of the city'. Later campaign materials referred to 'low-wage women', 'community women', 'low-income families' and 'low-income people', terms which were typical of the discourse of social analysis and political demand which developed during the campaign. A key element of this discourse was a consciousness of class, expressed in the leaflets, public meetings and other media, which contrasted the just demands of working people for affordable health care with the oppressive behaviour of middle-class professionals (Morgen, 1988: 103–4, 108).

One of the strongest points of contention in the campaign was a plan to replace the clinics with care provided by private doctors. Activists and community people argued that the sliding-scale fees in the clinics had provided 'affordable and dignified' health care; they also spoke of the 'relaxed atmosphere' of the clinics, where they were treated like 'real people' by the non-physician staff. This was contrasted with the demeaning and charitable flavour of the doctors' private provision. As one woman put it, 'We aren't second-class citizens at the clinics like we are for private doctors.'

The discourse of rights and demands of the activists clashed with the professional discourse of the doctors and hospital administrators, who spoke of the 'inability of consumers to judge what is quality health care' and who declared that they would not respond to 'demands, arguments, sneering, or being told what to do'. The loss of sliding-scale fees and ancillary services was redefined by the professionals as 'a sacrifice you ladies are just going to have to make'. At a crucial public meeting such statements led to the temporary ejection of the professionals. The activists, now in control of the meeting, railed against the 'callous', 'disrespectful' and 'insensitive' behaviour of the professionals who were seen as being motivated by greed and as thinking of the women as 'stupid and unworthy of having [their] views taken seriously'.

But the activists did not respond to the professionals in a monolithic way. There was a crucial debate among them over the use of the word 'demands', which some women wanted to drop, fearing that it was 'alienating' the professionals. Two events kept 'demand' in the activists' vocabulary. One was a statement by a doctor in a radio interview that he was pleased to see 'urge' replacing 'demand' in a petition because this showed that the campaigners were learning that they could not make demands of doctors. The other was a nurse saying to activists during a hearing on the dispute, 'You don't "demand" of doctors. You wouldn't make demands on your husbands.' This statement set off considerable discussion among the activists about women's rights to make demands of both doctors and husbands.

The clash of the professional and activist discourses set up a dynamic which was highly educative for the activists, who began to analyse both the vocabulary of the professionals, especially key words like 'provider' and 'consumer', and to understand how the strategy of defining political issues as medical ones maintained the professionals' dominance and obscured relations of class, gender and race. Their experience of the micro-politics of the campaign was also crucial in raising the activists' consciousness. The activists forced the health establishment to set up a task force to investigate the impact of the clinic closures. Initially, the activists were treated with contempt by the task force. At public hearings, the testimony of doctors and other professionals was not interrupted, while activists were repeatedly interrupted by the chair of the task force, a wealthy female lawyer. The activists were questioned about their sources of information and frequently requested to refrain from telling 'anecdotes' and 'personal stories'. At one hearing the task force chair expressed her disbelief that any woman who 'really wanted a baby' would be deterred by the cost of prenatal care and suggested that there 'must be a cultural gap at work here'. Soon after this remark, the activists withdrew from the hearing to decide how to respond to this contemptuous treatment. They returned with a prepared statement which identified the constant interruptions to activists' testimony as 'an attempt to intimidate us, to keep us from using what we know best, the experiences of real women'. The statement also named the class and gendered nature of the hearing process: 'This meeting is middle- and upper-class people making decisions about low-income people without understanding our needs at all.' The 'cultural gap' identified by the chair, the statement went on, was 'really an income gap'. The sexist attempt to label women's expressions of their experiences as 'gossip' was challenged in discussion among the activists but not publicly. 'That's what they think of women', said one activist.

As the campaign progressed, the activists' understanding of the class nature of the struggle in which they were engaged deepened, and their tactics became more sophisticated and confrontational. Dissatisfied with their treatment at task-force hearings, the activists forced the hospital board to see them. They were told that they would be given twenty minutes and could bring no more than four representatives to the meeting. The activists responded by organising a demonstration of more than one hundred community members outside the hospital as the board met. When the board refused to comply with any of the activists' demands, the four representatives addressed the public meeting which then invaded the office of the local newspaper to protest its failure to cover the demonstration. This brought the activists the publicity they sought. During the next month they kept the pressure on the hospital board through a petition, a letter-writing campaign, visits to other community organisations and local radio shows and by researching and publicising the social backgrounds of members of the hospital board, who were revealed to be overwhelmingly white, male and middle class. These actions enabled the activists to understand, as one of them put it, that 'this struggle is not just with the doctors and the hospital; it's the whole power of the city against us'.

## Edison High

When she was working as an adult educator in Philadelphia in the late 1970s, Wendy Luttrell (1988) was commissioned to develop a curriculum guide on 'women and the community' for adult basic education classes. As she gathered data for this guide, people kept referring to an ongoing struggle over the local high school. Edison High was located in a Philadelphia neighbourhood which had been deserted by white working-class families and increasingly populated by Hispanics and blacks. The whites literally took the neighbourhood high school, North Eastern High, with them, leaving behind an ageing building which was renamed Edison High. This school had the highest drop-out rate in the city and had the largest number of former students killed in the Vietnam war. For twenty years black and Hispanic parents unsuccessfully lobbied the white-controlled city government for a new high school to replace Edison. One of the reasons for the failure of these efforts was that white parents could send their children out of the area to other, more affluent, schools. In 1979 this option was closed off, forcing white parents into an alliance with blacks and Hispanics. A local anti-poverty group brokered the establishment of a largely female Coalition for a New High School which, over the next several years, successfully fought for the establishment of a new high school.

Luttrell's paper focuses on the female Coalition members' political experiences, and particularly on 'the interwoven relationship of gender, race and class consciousness' (Luttrell, 1988: 152). Coalition members spoke of how they had learned in the campaign about both their common interests with other racial groups and the ways in which local power brokers deliberately kept members of different ethnic groups fearful of and separated from each other. As one white woman put it, before the formation of the Coalition, even though she was very conscious of her children's need for proper schooling, she 'didn't know what to do. I just never had had anything to do with Black and Puerto Rican people before.' As another woman explained, when the various ethnic groups got together,

> we found out that we all wanted the same things for our children. ... As a white mother, because of my own prejudice, I had thought that black and Hispanic parents would settle for something a little less for their kids, that if I joined with them I might have to compromise something for my kids. I learned I was wrong.

A long-time local black activist spoke of how 'working with the coalition really made me challenge my own prejudices about white people. ... I have really learned that poverty knows no colour. We do share the same problems.'

In the course of the struggle over the high school these women un-learned racism, and learned solidarity. Like the activists in the struggle over the gynaecological clinic, the Edison women also learned about how people who hold power think, behave and can be influenced. One woman spoke of how at each public meeting, city officials

> set you up as you walk in. You can just see them looking at you up and down saying, 'What do these dames know; this is going to be a breeze'. Then when you start talking, throwing statistics at them, exposing the facts, you can see their attitudes change in minutes. They can't believe that these chicks who just walked in the room are strong, individual, and intelligent women. What really surprises these men is that we women can stand just as firmly on our positions as they can.

Two other Edison activists spoke of how they had learned that women do all the things that men get paid to do, and more.

Women have to change roles all the time. At one instant we are dealing with our children and keeping them together; then we switch to meetings, talking on the level of administrators. Afterwards we go right into the community and explain what happened in language everybody understands. Then, at night, we go home and explain it to our kids.

In contrast to this, men had only one role: they were lawyers or administrators, and they only had to deal with each other. The women felt that their multiple roles made them stronger leaders.

Luttrell's paper shows the complexity of the development of these women's political learning, which as she notes 'was not a linear process that in retrospect the women can identify with ease' (1988: 147). For a start, there were multiple sources of learning for these women, of which the experience of the Edison campaign was but one. Other sources included participation in a women's neighbourhood centre, adult education classes and significant life experiences like divorce. And it is likely that, as with my own neighbourhood house and rainforest campaign studies (Chapters 3 and 4, this volume), the research process itself provided an opportunity for the women Luttrell interviewed to articulate their learning, to make it explicit. Again, the women's developing political awareness did not simply free them to act. Coalition members' learning brought them up against the structural constraints of a racist society. With their new awareness of the common interests of working people, these women still had to live in a society founded on institutionalised racism, and they expressed an awareness of the difficulties of this. One white woman spoke of how hard she found it to act on her knowledge of racism in her own neighbourhood where people could not see 'how racism hurts them', and who didn't 'want to hear about it – even if it means their kids lose out'. For all the discussion in 'meeting after meeting' about how 'white people have to understand that their own racism is keeping them back', it was hard for this woman to go back to her community and have her new-found consciousness isolate her from her neighbours, friends and family. Yet, she said, she 'couldn't go back to thinking the way [she] used to'.

And yet in this complexity the Edison activists *did* act and learn in emancipatory ways. Like the Australian and Brazilian women whose struggles will be discussed later in this book, the Edison activists developed ways of acting and learning built on values of affiliation, nurturance, embeddedness in community, the collective good and the future of their children. In this learning and action these women challenged core values and processes of capitalism, including bureaucratic domination, class domination, patriarchy and racism. This is not to romanticise the women's learning, or to understate the complexities and ambiguities of their struggle, but to recognise its nature and importance.

## The insurance company

The third study to be reviewed here also demonstrates the relationship of social structure, ideology and discourse in emancipatory learning. In particular, it raises the issue of the determination of local struggles by wider economic and political forces, an issue that will be discussed in detail in subsequent chapters.

Costello (1988) examines a strike by female clerical employees of a small insurance company owned by a teachers' union. In the mid-1970s the business of this company grew rapidly. Management responded to this expansion by hiring more clerical staff, moving some staff to a new location and tightening management control over the clerical work process. A time clock was installed, and workers were rebuked for being even a minute late. Clerical staff were directed to use a side door and the firestair, leaving the front door and elevator free for management use. A rigid system of lunch breaks was introduced. Supervisors monitored workers' telephone calls, issued written reprimands for talking, refused to grant leave for family responsibilities to women workers, and even followed workers to the lavatory.

These changes coincided with the organisation of the workplace by a clerical workers' union, which had already found management uncooperative in negotiations over an initial workplace contract. The ill-feeling generated by the new, harsh management practices led to the emergence of more assertive tactics by workers. During negotiations over a second contract in 1979, workers developed a militant discourse, at the heart of which were notions of workers' and women's rights. 'Management has no empathy or even insight into the problems we, as women, face when combining jobs and homemaking', the workers' newsletter reported. When management interpreted as 'cluttering up the contract' the union's attempt to include issues relating to 'employee rights', the workers' newsletter explicitly referred to the conflict between the two discourses: 'We, however, are unwavering;

our concept of contract language is of equal importance to that of management.'

As the negotiations progressed, relationships between union and management became increasingly confrontational and it appeared that a strike was inevitable. Clerical workers used existing friendship networks to spread information about the strike, clandestinely making use of the internal telephone and mail systems. At the heart of the women's militancy were feelings of solidarity and a demand that management treat them with dignity and respect. Stories of management indignities were diffused throughout the workplace, making the women more determined. 'When one woman becomes upset, everyone becomes upset', one woman said. 'This feeding off each other was what started the strike.' 'We felt we weren't going to be pushed around anymore', said another woman. 'Management was not acting respectful toward our bargaining team. So we decided to stand up for our rights!'

The women also waged a struggle within their own union, which was dominated by male professionals wedded to formal and legalistic procedures which alienated the female clerical workers. 'The professionals had a technique for talking above the union women's heads', one interviewee commented. 'It gives you the impression that they know more than they do. They dominated.' The women took advantage of a union rule allowing different groups of workers to conduct their own meetings, which the clerical workers then did, using the informal ties and language of their own work culture. As the day of the strike vote approached, all 53 women assembled at a local hotel. When the two male union officials negotiating on the women's behalf reached a settlement with management without consulting their members, the women unanimously voted to strike.

The two-month strike deepened the women's militancy. Freed from the constraints of workplace hierarchy, the women continued to act assertively. On the picket line, popular supervisors were treated lightly, while arrogant managers were insulted and ridiculed. The women wrote songs and chants satirising management. The strike released the clerical workers from their accustomed constraints and enabled them to express their anger at management. As one striker put it, all the women 'got crazy occasionally', they 'got loud and rowdy, held up nasty signs, and said things they usually wouldn't say'. Some of the women also defied their husbands who had demanded that they quit the strike. On warmer days, some of the women brought their children with them to the picket line, an act which, according to one striker, 'management resented because it made them look bad'. And the strikers defied their employer, the teachers' union, by getting the film star Jane Fonda, who was the keynote speaker at the union's annual convention, to work into her speech a statement of the women's grievances. 'What if I told you', Fonda began, to the audience of 5,000 teachers, 'that there are 53 women who work for an insurance company, who, like Blacks in the days when they had to sit in the back of the buses, aren't allowed to walk in the front of the building and take an elevator to their offices?', and went on to list the striker's grievances, finishing with: 'And what if I told you that they're *your* employees.' The union leadership was furious; for the women it was the high point of the strike, gaining them publicity and legitimising their actions.

After two months, with their money running out, the women accepted a contract which won them some of their demands, including access to the front door and elevator, the firing of three managers and the replacement of a particularly disliked male personnel manager by a woman manager. Looking back, the women felt that their main gain from the strike was an understanding of their rights as working women. As one woman put it,

> Before the strike I would have done whatever I was told, not thinking I had the right to say otherwise. Now I do realise that ... if you are not getting treated equally and fairly, you do have the right to say otherwise. ... I learned not to be afraid. ... [Before the strike] I felt like I was stepping on pins and needles all the time. ... I learned I didn't have to take that anymore.

But over the next two years management introduced new strategies of control which eroded the power the workers had gained. Several strike leaders were promoted to supervisory positions, a psychologist was brought in to gather information about worker and management perceptions, a monthly luncheon was introduced at which workers could air grievances, and training workshops and discussion groups were initiated to facilitate management–worker communication. At the same time, claims processing was made more automated, decreasing workers' control over their work and introducing a machine-based method of measuring worker productivity.

By the time of the next contract negotiations, in 1982, these changes had combined with high staff turnover, the onset of a national and global economic recession and a national swing to political conservatism, to radically reduce the militancy of the clerical workers. With some of the workers' initial grievances met, some of their leaders coopted, 'softer' forms of supervision dividing the workforce, and a new way of monitoring productivity introduced, management had regained its dominance. A strike leader encapsulated the outcome of the struggle for control of this workplace, and the role of competing discourses in the struggle, when she said, 'Ultimately, management could implement work rules around production standards. ... That would kill us. ... With the previous [contract] language, management couldn't have done this'.

\* \* \*

The three studies discussed in this chapter demonstrate how central the struggle between insurgent and dominant discourses is to emancipatory learning in social action. They also show that emancipatory struggle is not straightforwardly developmental and inevitably triumphant. Gains can be, and often are, reversed.

The nature of the learning that occurs in hegemonic struggle has certain broad commonalities. In this chapter we have seen women in three different situations gain self-confidence and useful skills and knowledge, and develop a critical understanding of how power works in society. Above all, we have witnessed people learning that they *could* act, and learning that the action that they took made a difference.

These three studies also illustrate the diverse and complex nature of struggles between resistant and dominant discourses. It is vital to understand the distinctive ways hegemonic struggle plays itself out in particular instances of social action. While important lessons can be learned from other struggles, there are no formulas; as the case studies in the following chapters demonstrate in greater detail, each struggle has its unique dynamic.

Another commonality in the instances of social action discussed in this book is that they all took place within capitalist societies. While some of the ways in which broader economic and political forces shape local struggles have been noted, the ways in which capitalism *determines* emancipatory struggle and learning have not been discussed in any detail. This is a theme to which I will return later in the book.

# CHAPTER 3

# Learning in a Green Campaign

I turn now to a more extended analysis of learning in social action. This chapter examines a successful campaign to preserve a rainforest remnant in the Terania Creek basin in eastern Australia. The first section sketches the social and ecological setting of Terania Creek and gives a brief chronology of the events of the campaign. Then follows a narrative account of the campaign from the perspective of some of its key participants. The final section of the chapter discusses the learning that took place in the Terania Creek campaign.

## Setting and chronology

Terania Creek is a 700-hectare remnant of what was a 75,000 hectare rainforest on the east coast of Australia. 'New settlers', urban, middle-class people, began to move into the region in the early 1970s. As a group, the new settlers wanted to develop a self-sufficient, ecologically sound and often communal way of life. These aims, together with other sub-cultural differences (dress, music, spiritual life) distinguished them from, and often aroused the antipathy of, the older settlers (dairy farmers, timber workers), government workers and business people. (See Watson, 1990: 38–62 for an extended discussion of the culture of north-coast timber workers, and Metcalfe, 1986, for the values of the new settlers.)

Soon after settling in the area, the new settlers learned that the Forestry Commission intended to log the Terania Creek basin. The Forestry Commission argued that only 'old growth' eucalypt forest would be cut, with minimal disturbance to rainforest species. This did not reassure the new settlers, who were convinced that eucalypt and rainforest were in symbiosis, and that to extract one would destroy the other.

A small group of new settlers formed an action group and for the five years 1974–79 lobbied the Forestry Commission and the New South Wales State Government to try to prevent the logging. In August 1979 the Forestry Commission tried to commence logging the Terania rainforest remnant. Several hundred new settlers engaged in non-violent direct action for several weeks, severely hampering the logging operation. The State Government then placed a moratorium on logging at Terania Creek and appointed a commission of enquiry. The commission's report was released in February 1982 and found in favour of logging. The Government did not act on the report and six months later incorporated the Terania Creek rainforest in the new Nightcap National Park.

## The campaign

The following account of the Terania Creek campaign is a severely condensed version of an account (Foley, 1991a) based on the recollections of five people who were deeply involved in the campaign, supplemented by contemporary newspaper and other print materials. Taped interviews with the activists were carried out in August and September 1990, and the transcripts of the interviews were subsequently checked by the respondents.

The Terania Creek campaign began as a spontaneous reaction by new settlers to the imminent destruction of the environment that had attracted them to settle. Nan Nicholson was active in the Terania Creek campaign and now, with her husband Hugh, runs a rainforest nursery at Terania Creek. Nan recalls that when the new settlers learned that the Forestry Commission was planning to log the Terania basin:

> we were very alarmed, because we'd made this naive assumption that it looked nice now and it was going to stay that way. ... So we really sprang into action after that with a lot of fear. We had no idea how to go about a campaign, we just knew we wanted to stop it. It was a real knee-jerk reaction.

A small group of new settlers soon formed the Terania Native

Forest Action Group (TNFAG), the organisation that was to carry out the campaign. From 1975 to 1979 the activists gathered information, lobbied the Forestry Commission and the State Government, publicised the issue through public meetings, songs and a television advertisement, and used various other tactics.

We tried everything, we invited the [national] Museum up and had field studies done. We did a transect ourselves across the forest and noted every tree and had them identified and so produced our own profiles of the forest. ... We took Aboriginal people up there to look at sites that we found, and had the National Parks archaeological section do transects through a big cave that's up there, looking for previous habitation. There were significant finds two metres down, it had been an important site for Aborigines, apparently they used it for male initiation. (Michael Murphy, 19/8/90)

In the years from 1974 to 1979 the core group of Terania Creek activists – ten to fifteen people – learned a lot about the dynamics of campaigning: about the need for accurate knowledge and persistence, about the need to vary tactics, about the importance of identifying the real decision-makers. There is also evidence of a deeper sort of learning, to do with the activists becoming clearer about their own, and their opponents', values and strategies:

We certainly learned a lot, mainly the courage to stand up to politicians. We had been imbued with this idea that the experts really know what they're talking about and that judges are honest and that politicians are basically there because they like people and want to do something for the state. But all these ideas came tumbling down really quickly. The first one to come tumbling down was this idea that the foresters were experts and they knew what they were doing and knew how to manage forests. That might actually be the case, but the political pressures on the foresters are huge. In the Terania campaign these came out immediately ...

Our initial reaction was an emotional one, 'This is beautiful, what you're going to do is terrible!' But subsequently we started investigating the facts and began to find out that there wasn't much rainforest left, and that there were a few other reasons for preserving it, apart from the fact that it was pretty. And so we really started gathering opinions then, contacting people like Professor Webb from Queensland who's a rainforest ecologist, and beginning to get a lot more information under our belts. I think we became a lot more threatening then. The more informed we became the more they backed off, hoping we would go away ...

They thought we were unreasonable because they thought they had compromised along the way. But from my point of view we reached the point way past balance decades ago. What we're fighting over now are these tiny little remnants, and talking about attacking them to me is absolute extremism. So if I want to defend them I'm being conservative, I'm not being extreme. But the foresters could not understand that ...

There wasn't any issue about money. There wasn't even an issue about jobs. It was such a tiny little area. It was about three months' work for a few blokes. It wasn't about jobs, it was about expertise and a very entrenched bureaucracy being tackled by so-called upstarts. And that's a really deep emotional issue to them so they say that we're emotionalists and they're into facts and objectivity. But from my point of view it was clear it *was* about emotions, it was about them being challenged. The other point was that our group was half women and they'd never had women taking the initiative. So there was all this complex stuff going on. (Nan Nicholson, 26/9/90)

In the period 1974 to 1979 the Terania action group was small, highly committed and self-financing.

... we had a lot of fun. I'm sure now that's the absolute crux of doing anything in life at all. Basically, it is about maintaining the humour level. Because if you don't do that, who wants to go to a meeting? – it's boring and full of doom. (Ibid.)

Meetings were run

very informally. We had no formal secretary, I think we called Michael (Murphy) secretary, but that was only because he had a typewriter. ... The initial period was certainly exhausting, but we all felt that we were getting enough out of it to keep on going. It was a good feeling of being right. (Ibid.)

Initially the campaign was funded out of the activists'

own pockets. None of us were rich and we just kept forking out little bits all the time. In fact, one of our members was really in difficulty with his land repayments. So we started clubbing together to help pay them, because he was a very effective publicist. ... We weren't getting much support from the Sydney folk [i.e. conservation groups] at that time. They came into it quite belatedly. I think there was a lot of prejudice about hippies in the hills. (Ibid.)

Eventually, however, two influential Sydney-based green organisations threw their weight behind the campaign, bringing with them valuable legal and scientific expertise. Also, 'just by creating enough of a stir money started to come in. Our biggest donation was $5,000, which we just couldn't believe.' (Ibid.)

As with the beginning of the campaign, the protesters' move to direct action in August 1979 was spontaneous, a reaction to the Forestry Commission's announcement that it was to commence logging immediately.

> We never actually planned at all for any of this direct action stuff. We had no strategy in place, no idea how to go about it. We'd talked about it a bit, but basically didn't want to think about it. (Nan Nicholson, 26/9/90)

> Luckily for us it happened on the weekend of the Channon market so we turned the market into a big rally and got lots of people involved. We started setting up a camp the next week. People started moving tents in and before we knew it we had about 200 people camping on the land right next to the forest on the last farm, which luckily for us was Hugh and Nan [Nicholson's] farm. (Michael Murphy, 19/8/90)

The campaigners were now faced with the question of how they were to organise themselves. They were anxious to avoid hierarchical forms of organisation. Three forms of organisation emerged in the camp: small functional groups, a coordinating body and a daily strategic meeting. The functional groups were identified by the colours of the rainbow: yellow for communications, purple for musicians and theatre, green for physical and mental well-being, red for transport and blue for kitchen and camp. In addition, there was a group responsible for liaising with the media and politicians. One person from each of the functional groups was appointed to a coordinating body. There was also a daily strategic meeting, to which all camp members could come, and at which the next day's strategy was discussed. Members of the coordinating body would report back both to their small groups and to the strategic meeting. One of the campaigners remembers that this structure and process 'made for a very intelligent head. What I liked about it most was that it was really consensus at work' (Ian Gaillard, 19/8/90; Carol Perry, 19/8/90).

But the organisation of the camp and the direct action were not without problems and dilemmas. The campers were a diverse group: 'you had the suited academics on the one hand, and the most ... druggie hippie on the other hand, and everything in between'. This diversity bred disagreement over tactics, and difficulties in decision-making. There were also tensions among the small groups, and between the small groups and the daily strategy meeting. The most noticeable difference was between the political-media group and the rest of the campers.

Nan Nicholson, a member of the political group, which was based in the Nicholsons' house, recalls that her group 'had to be wary that we didn't try to put ourselves over as an elite group, which would have been easy to do'. She also remembers that the 'political bunch' would have what were, in effect, committee meetings in her house and then would go to the strategy meeting 'and tell them what was happening or else they'd come and tell us. It sounds hierarchical, but it wasn't. We certainly attempted to make sure that it wasn't. But I guess in the end you do have a bit of a problem because there are always the people at the bottom level of information who don't know a lot about it.'

A decade later, Nan Nicholson's response to the tension that developed in the campaign between openness and effectiveness, and between consensus decision-making and flexible and creative tactics was to assert the primacy of openness, and to accept the inevitability of the tensions.

> I've learnt now to live with problems that are insoluble. I just feel that you can't expect to have everything right and you can't wait to be happy, wait for the problems to be gone to be happy. So you've got to be able to live with that one. It's a hard lesson to learn. Certainly there was a lot of effort put into informing everybody. [But] it's too much to expect that everybody should know everything. I feel comfortable with that … (Nan Nicholson, 26/9/90)

The direct action phase of the campaign created other difficulties. One of these related to the intensity and stress generated by the campaign. The political group operated from the Nicholsons' 'twenty foot by twenty foot one-roomed house'.

> That's where Hugh and I were living, but there were also about 20 others at various times living in and around that house, on the verandah, and half the time we didn't even know what they were doing. You'd hear the gestetner machine and the typewriter just going all night and we didn't even know what they were doing. We had little kids at the time too. So it was a stressful time but I was really aware then that it was something really historic and it was just something that I had to put my whole being into and hang with it and not pull out and say, 'I can't cope with this'. (Ibid.)

The protesters' camp was established over the weekend of 11 and 12 August, 1979. The protesters knew that the Forestry Commission intended to use a bulldozer to reopen the old logging road to the north of the Nicholsons' property, and in preparation they blockaded an access road with old cars. Ian Gaillard remembers 'walking past twenty cars, and they were jacked up with their wheels taken off in a line on this narrow road. The people went up past the cars and there was a lot of music. Music was a very strong part of it, a lot of musicians were there from the local area. I think they were singing *We Shall Not Be Moved.*'

On Friday 17 August the bulldozer was moved down the logging road, escorted by police. The police and private tow-truck operators removed the cars blocking the road. When the cars had been removed, the protesters put themselves in the path of the bulldozer:

> Just walking really slowly in front of the bulldozer, just being a mass of people. There always seemed to be a mass of people just there, their hand on the blade and eyeballing the driver and saying, 'You can't go any further'. And all the time one of the themes that kept emerging from the camp circles was: talk to the police, this is a non-violent action, let's keep it that way, let's talk with the police, tell them the story of why this forest shouldn't be logged, and keep it down. And because of this structure of the different colour groups, each time a group went into the forest a musician would go, and a person from health and well-being, to be with the group. I remember having a red cross on and completely bamboozling the police saying, 'Look, I've got a red cross, I have to go in there', and we'd have a back-pack full of food for the people who were up the trees. (Ian Gaillard, 19/8/90)

The police made seventeen arrests on the first day of the confrontation.

> It was a stand-off that first night. Our numbers had swelled, because we had a telephone tree which had been activated. So suddenly, from 200 people, we had 300 people in an hour or so. The additional people were all local people. (Michael Murphy, 19/8/90)

At the end of the first week of direct action the bulldozer had moved one-third of the way along the old logging track, and no logging had occurred. There followed a four-day interregnum during which the police and the loggers withdrew and in the protesters camp 'there were lots of ideas, plans and much merriment'. The loggers' bulldozer was sabotaged twice by some protesters and repaired by other campers who felt that such sabotage would alienate public support for the campaign. Then, early in the morning of Wednesday 22 August, '130 police arrived in 20 cars, 5 wagons, 1 bus, 3 tow trucks and one rescue squad vehicle. ... At 10am 40 police accompanied a dozer, which ... cut a path to the forest centre' (*Nimbin News*, 27/8/79).

Once the road had been 'bulldozed into the forest itself, work groups made entry difficult for paddy-wagons picking up arrestees by digging trenches across the track, diverting water channels into log-holes and levering boulders into place' (Nan Nicholson, 1982: 38). 'With the road through the forest moving into virgin country we decided on climbing trees with some people on the ground, as the best way of slowing down the progress' (*Nimbin News*, 27/8/79). Some of the tree climbers 'sat in trees below those about to be felled. Some strung wire cables between trees ... .' Others slung 'hammocks up in the trees, they could stay there for days at a time' (Nan Nicholson, 1982: 39; Michael Murphy, 19/8/90).

These tactics slowed the logging considerably. But once into the logging area:

> The foresters started to knock the trees down pretty quickly. They were starting to move a whole group of men with saws in and log the lot and then worry about pulling them out later. ... It was a very hasty operation. There are still a lot of trees up there that landed on top of each other and smashed each other to pieces and so it was a total waste of trees. If you go up there today it's very hard to walk through that section. (Michael Murphy, 19/8/90)

While the confrontation in the forest was going on, members of TNFAG periodically visited Sydney to try to persuade the New South Wales State Cabinet to discuss the issue. But access to Cabinet was difficult, partly because of the determined advocacy of the loggers' case by the Minister responsible for the Forestry Commission, Lyn Gordon, and partly because the State Premier, Neville Wran, had yet to be convinced that the Terania Creek protesters had significant public support. Paradoxically, it was an 'extreme' action that the Terania campers had decided *not* to take, that halted the logging:

> It was individualists who cut up the felled timber into 6ft lengths and hammered spikes into standing trees [leaving warning signs]. These tactics had been discussed at length in the camp and a strong consensus decision

made not to risk the rebound of public alienation. After the discovery of such dastardly acts, TNFAG immediately informed the millowners and released press statements denouncing the damage but taking responsibility for it. Although publicly disowned by the protesters, the perpetrators could take credit for having effectively halted the logging. The loggers' tactic of hurried felling without waiting for removal of the logs would have had the whole area down within a few days and the vandalism to the logs forced them to abandon that policy. The most questionable acts and those which lost a great deal of public support, actually saved the day. (Nan Nicholson, 1982: 45)

The logging of Terania Creek was halted on Friday 31 August 1979, twenty days after the establishment of the protesters' camp (*DN*, 30/8/79; *NS*, 3/9/79; Prineas and Elenius, n.d.: 2). The Terania Creek rainforest was not to be logged again. But the campaign to save the forest was to go on for almost three years after the cessation of logging.

There was an immediate backlash against the halting of logging (*NS*, 30/8/79). After the logging halted, the protesters maintained a small group of people at the camp on the Nicholsons' property. On 7 September the Lismore City Council ordered the closure of the camp, claiming that 'lack of adequate sanitary facilities' had created 'a nuisance prejudicial to health'. On the same evening as the council meeting, a sawmill in Lismore was burnt to the ground (*NS*, 8/9/90). The conservationists were accused of having set the fire, and they in turn suspected that the mill might have been torched to discredit them, at a time when the Government was making its decision on the Terania logging.

The Terania campaign polarised the region. On one side were the conservationists, most of them new settlers. On the other side were the logging interests (millowners, forestry workers and the bureaucrats servicing the timber industry), local business people, many farmers, and, initially, the three major political parties. The new settlers felt this polarisation sharply (see Foley, 1991a: 28–30). Throughout the Terania Creek campaign local mass media opposed the conservationists, who were portrayed as self-indulgent and economically irresponsible hippies and 'dole bludgers' (*DN*, 31/8/79; *NS*, 1/9/79). The timber lobby was also active throughout the campaign, putting out publicity and lobbying local and State Governments (*NS*, 3/9/79 and *NS*, 4/9/79).

The antipathy of some local workers and business people towards the conservationists often had an economic basis. In the years following World War Two, mechanisation, mergers and national economic crisis and restructuring caused a long-term decline in employment in the timber industry, with the number of workers falling from 8,200 in 1939 to 1,038 in 1971 (Watson, 1990: 1–9, 51–2). In the 1970s this process accelerated, with large sawmills buying out smaller ones, 'in order to obtain their crown log quotas. They then closed down the mills and sold off the equipment' (Watson, 1990: 8). In this situation, the conservationists' demand that logging be halted at Terania Creek was threatening to both local workers and business people.

The Terania campaigners tried, but failed, to convince timber workers that logging native forests was futile, 'that they were logging this resource to extinction [and that] they were going to be out of a job in ten years anyway' (Nan Nicholson, 26/9/90; cf. Michael Murphy, 19/8/90). As one of the conservationists later realised, neither spiritual nor economic arguments against logging 'make sense to someone who's talking about his kids and his job. And you especially can't tell him that his job is going to be gone in ten years anyway, he doesn't want to hear that stuff, he's worried about right now. So it's really hard stuff to argue' (Nan Nicholson, 26/9/90). (This point is dealt with at length in Watson, 1990.) The conservationists were also reluctant to approach loggers because of the bitterness generated by the campaign (Foley, 1991a: 31–2).

The suspension of logging at Terania Creek was followed by a visit from a six-member sub-committee of the State Cabinet, and then, two weeks later, from a sub-committee of the State Labour Party Caucus. (*NT*, 22/9/79). The conservationists took full opportunity to put their views on Terania Creek to the politicians. A member of TNFAG, who had been lobbying in Sydney, was on the same plane as the Cabinet sub-committee and distributed information kits on Terania Creek to the politicians. The Cabinet delegation was greeted at the local airport by a crowd of conservationists 'saying "Welcome, thanks for coming, glad to see you" and saying what a great area it was, and it shouldn't be logged, and not abusing politicians' (Michael Murphy, 19/8/90). In contrast, when the Caucus delegation arrived at Casino the loggers organised a demonstration 'that was full of abuse, calling politicians hippie lovers and all that stuff'. The conservationists 'made sure we did not abuse politicians, and I think that worked in our favour. ... We just tried to keep aware that politicians are human as well, even though we felt so cynical about their motives' (Nan Nicholson, 26/9/90).

In the course of the campaign the Terania Creek activists learned a lot about how to work with politicians, about the need for sensitivity, flexibility and, above all, persistence.

> *When you went down to Sydney, those two times (during the Terania Creek blockade), did you actually get to talk to [Premier] Wran or other people?*
> M: Finally we got through his door, after trying for many months.
> *What was that like?*
> M: We couldn't get past his minders before that, but then finally the events up there were the first item up on the news, and so it suddenly became a hot issue for them.
> *So he realised he had to do something?*
> Yes, his door was always open, he said: 'My door is always open' (laughs).
> I: He'd say that to the media, as he said goodbye he'd say: 'Come and see me anytime, my door is always open' (laughs).
> M: We'd spent months sitting outside that door trying to talk to the man. It was crazy. (Michael Murphy and Ian Gaillard, 19/8/90. For more in this vein, see Foley, 1991a: 33–5)

In 1979 the New South Wales Government appointed a retired Supreme Court Judge, Simon Isaacs, to conduct an enquiry into the proposed logging of Terania Creek. The enquiry went on for nearly two years, received 128 submissions and 343 exhibits, heard 67 witnesses and cost $1 million, paid out of the Forestry Commission's budget. This was for timber that would have gained the State Government, in the estimate of the Forestry Commission, $31,314 in royalties (*NS*, 15/2/82; Prineas and Elenius, n.d.: 1, 6; Hugh Nicholson, 26/9/90).

The conservationists are convinced that Wran appointed the enquiry in order to take the heat out of the Terania Creek confrontation and, possibly, to give him time to build up the numbers so he would win a vote on the issue in a Cabinet that contained pro-logging interests. The conservationists remember the enquiry as an 'horrific' and 'exhausting' experience. The environmentalists were disadvantaged at the enquiry, in several ways. With the end of the confrontation in the forest, the work of continuing the campaign fell back on the core group of TNFAG activists, who could not match the resources of the timber industry and the Forestry Commission. (Michael Murphy, 19/8/90; Nan and Hugh Nicholson, 26/9/90).

According to the environmentalists, the conduct of the enquiry also disadvantaged them. Judge Isaacs was an old man, and not in good health, so the bulk of the enquiry was conducted on 'the tenth floor of a high-rise in Sydney', remote in distance and atmosphere from the forest whose fate was being decided. The judge also appeared to the conservationists to interpret the enquiry's terms of reference in a narrow and legalistic way, which favoured the pro-logging interests (Prineas and Elenius, n.d.: 3–4; Ian Gaillard and Michael Murphy, 19/8/90). The judge's preference for narrow 'scientific' and 'objective' analysis over an holistic, ecological and committed approach to forestry also worked against the conservationists' (Foley, 1991a: 37–8).

The report of the Terania Creek enquiry was released in February 1982. It recommended that Terania Creek continue to be logged for another five years and that logging should then be stopped for 25 years, an insufficient time, according to conservationists, for rainforest regeneration. The State Government did not release the Isaacs report until six months after it had been written. This may have been because Wran was waiting for the development of anti-logging public opinion to convince Cabinet that to log would be to lose votes (Hugh Nicholson, 26/9/90). Certainly, the day the Isaacs report was released a public opinion poll showed that 69 per cent of voters opposed further rainforest logging (*NS*, 12/2/82). Several months later the New South Wales Cabinet decided that Terania Creek would become part of the Nightcap National Park.

While the Isaacs enquiry was in progress the conservationists continued to educate politicians and the public about the rainforest issue, through film and print. Beginnings were also made on rainforest reafforestation, at first in conjunction with the State Government, and when the Forestry Commission refused to cooperate, independently. These efforts led to the launching of a programme of reafforestation and education that was still under way a decade later, and the establishment by the Nicholsons of a rainforest nursery, which, by the early 1990s, had supplied 250,000 seedlings to the tropical east coast of Australia and produced a number of books on rainforest plants (Michael Murphy and Ian Gaillard, 19/8/90; Hugh and Nan Nicholson, 26/9/90).

## Learning

The table on pp. 40–5 summarises what the five activists who were interviewed learned in the Terania Creek campaign. The quotations in the right-hand column of the table, and the numbers in brackets, are, in the main, from the paper on which this chapter is based (Foley, 1991a).

The learning of activists in the Terania Creek campaign was significant, in two related ways. First, in the campaign, activists acquired new skills and knowledge. They developed considerable expertise in rainforest ecology, expertise that they continued to use subsequently. They developed understanding of the State and its agents (public servants, politicians, judges), and skills in working with and acting on it. They acquired analogous understanding and skills in relation to the mass media. They also developed skills in, and an understanding of the complexities of, building democratic forms of organisation and taking direct action.

But there is another dimension of learning in the campaign, which relates to what Freire (1972a: 75–83) called conscientisation, and Mezirow (1981) named perspective transformation. The experience of the campaign challenged and significantly altered the campaigners' understanding of the world. The activists moved from assuming that the value of the rainforest was self-evident to learning that it was something that had to be struggled for. Their initial faith in experts and authority was replaced by an understanding of some of the ways in which expertise and authority are embedded in social interests, power relations and epistemologies (forms of knowledge, ways of understanding). Finally, the activists learned that they could acquire expertise, build new forms of organisation, take action and change things.

These learnings are significant and empowering. They are also incidental to, or embedded in, the action taken by the activists. The learnings were not articulated systematically at the time of the campaign or subsequently. We are talking here about *informal learning in social action*, or to put it in a more political way, *learning in the struggle*. This is an aspect of learning that has been paid too little attention by adult educators; it is a dimension of political action that has often been ignored by political activists. The neglect in both cases is understandable. Adult educators' time is taken up with teaching,

| Learning | Illustration |
|---|---|
| 1. Different forms of organisation emerged, these were informal, non-hierarchical and democratic. | We had no formal secretary (10). Three forms of organisation emerged in the camp ... (13). It was incredibly efficient, organised in this way, without a person being in charge ... (15) The group took responsibility for the group working well ... (15). |
| 2. Such forms of organisation involve the whole person and are creative and energising, in contrast with bureaucratic organisation which is contractual, alienating and reifying. | Right from the start the group got on really well because there was a great need for social interactions, and working together on this issue satisfied a lot of intellectual and emotional and spiritual needs for all of us ... (5). We just met together and always had food and cups of tea and stuff like that. It was really good fun (10). The camp just got more and more organised, it was a very exciting place to be ... (13). There were a lot of people who'd come here, there was a lot of creative energy at that time ... (16). That's why I said that it was a very intelligent head that was at work here. People listened to each other and acted upon each other's advice (16). We felt that we were up against people who were doing this because they were told to or because they were being paid. ... Often they seemed to be un-organised and not able to cope with our energy and the new tactics ... (10). |
| 3. But these new forms of organisation have their difficulties and ambiguities ... | But the decision-making was difficult. ... We all came from different extremes ... (17). ... [A]nd it did feel like a bit of separation between the camp and the people who worked as the spokespeople (17–18). It sounds hierarchical, but it |

| Learning | Illustration |
|---|---|
|  | wasn't. We certainly attempted to make sure that it wasn't. But I guess in the end you do have a bit of a problem … (18). Consensus is okay, but it never works totally. It's just that it's definitely better than a hierarchy … and that's why we had to have endless meetings. You just get really bored with meetings and really sick of it, but there seems to be no other way around it (19). |
| … and their unpredictable and unintended outcomes | This particular meeting was about whether we should cut up logs in the forest. … We in fact rejected the idea. … But then … some people decided to do it anyway … (20). |
| 4. A small group of committed and persistent people can make a difference. | There was probably only a core group of ten or fifteen (10). |
| 5. Commitment energises people. | Also we were prepared to work very long hours, which they found hard to understand, and they also couldn't understand how you could go on and on without money. We didn't know how we did that either – we just managed to (10–11). |
| 6. Activists can initially resource local campaigns. | Well, first it was just out of our own pockets. None of us were rich and we just kept forking out bits all the time (11). |
| 7. But for a sustained campaign other resources are necessary. | Two Sydney-based organisations … supported us a lot right from the start … (11). [At the enquiry] the environmentalists could not match the resources of the timber industry and the Forestry Commission (36). |
| 8. Keep the information coming. | We just put out information and kept circulating it … (21). |

| Learning | Illustration |
| --- | --- |
| 9. Use the mass media. | I'd also heard about a television advertisement ... (6). I guess that's what it is when you attract media attention: the politicians have to look ... (34). A film was made ... (38). |
| 10. Authorities can be influenced. | [The foresters] modified their proposed plans ... (8). I think the politicians were quite shocked to see what it was like (32). Finally we got through his door, after trying for many months (33). |
| 11. Expertise can be acquired. | But subsequently we started investigating the facts and began to find out that there wasn't much rainforest left. ... I think we became a lot more threatening then ... (8). |
| 12. Direct action is learned 'on the job'. | We never actually planned at all for any of this direct action stuff. We had no strategy in place, no idea how to go about it (12). |
| 13. Direct action is flexible and creative. | ... walking past twenty cars and they were jacked up with their wheels taken off. ... The people went up past the cars and there was a lot of music ... (22). Just walking really slowly in front of the bulldozer, just being a mass of people ... (22). ... [W]ork groups made entry difficult for paddy wagons. ... [W]e decided on climbing trees ... (24). ... [W]e'd try and stage events before a Cabinet meeting ... (25). ... [I]t was individualists also who cut up the felled brush box into 6 ft lengths and hammered spikes into standing trees ... (25). |

| Learning | Illustration |
|---|---|
| 14. Activism is stressful, it's important for activists to support each other. | It was very stressful. ... In hind-sight I think you'd need to be more skilful at ... really being able to talk to each other and help each other ... (21). |
| 15. Sustained and determined environmental action polarises a community and reveals social structures and interests. | The Terania campaign polarised the Northern Rivers ... (28). The law and order question was paramount ... (28). Lismore City Council, along with the local paper, the *Northern Star*, was the most frantic and illogical of the institutions threatened by the Terania Creek campaign ... (30, 26–27). The timber lobby was also active throughout the ... campaign ... (27). The antipathy of local people towards the conservationists often had an economic as well as a cultural basis ... (30). |
| 16. It is important, but difficult, for conservationists to try to understand the position of workers affected by a campaign, and to try to reach them. | You really have to make an attempt to talk to them and listen to them ... (31). That's a lot of our problem – people not being able to understand what we are doing (35) ... they couldn't put themselves up against authority ... (29). |
| 17. State-sponsored enquiries can work against activists. | The conservationists remember the enquiry as a 'horrific' and 'exhausting' experience (35). ... [T]he environmentalists could not match the resources of the timber industry and the Forestry Commission (36). ... [T]he enquiry was ... remote in distance and atmosphere from the forest whose fate was being decided ... (31). The judge interpreted the enquiry's terms of reference in a narrow and legalistic way ... (36). The way the judge heard evidence also disadvantaged the conservationists ... (36). |

| Learning | Illustration |
|---|---|
| 18. Significant learning involves people's assumptions being challenged, and is unsettling. | So we were very alarmed, because we'd made this naive assumption that it looked nice and it was going to stay that way (4). |
| 19. Expertise and authority are de-mystified in social action, and their social and historical contexts understood. | We had been imbued with this idea that the experts really know what they're talking about and that judges are honest and that politicians are basically there because they like people and want to do something for the state. But all these ideas came tumbling down really quickly (17). It was about emotions, it was about them being challenged ... (19). I think [the chief forester] felt very deeply that we should challenge him (8) ... and of course we were on opposing sides ... (7). It wasn't about jobs, it was about expertise and a very entrenched bureaucracy being tackled by so-called upstarts (9). Well, we learnt really early on ... that with the politician you always have to think of everything from his point of view ... and how what you're doing can help him ... (33). |
| 20. Conservationists and their opponents have such different ways of understanding the world that it may be impossible for them to communicate with each other. | ... in the 1920s the Forestry Commission knew that the forest was going to run out in the 1980s if they kept cutting it ... (7). ... [I]n that situation you're not talking about the same thing. So the enquiry is almost an impossibility, because you're coming from such different directions, there's almost no contact (37). ... [T]hey say that we're emotionalists and they're into facts and objectivity (9). ... [W]e are talking holistically ... about all the emotional values of forests, the ... values of forests ... (37). |

| Learning | Illustration |
| --- | --- |
| 21. In the course of a struggle activists become clearer about their values. | … this myth of objectivity … really concerns me, because it means that you reduce everything to things that can be measured … (37). They thought we were being unreasonable because they thought they had compromised along the way. But from my point of view we reached the point past balance decades ago. What we're fighting over now are these tiny little remnants, and talking about attacking them to me is absolute extremism. So if I want to defend them I'm being conservative, I'm not being extreme … (9). |

curriculum development, administration and, increasingly, with obtaining resources to keep programmes afloat. Activists, on the other hand, are primarily concerned with organisation and strategy around issues and campaigns.

Yet, as the Terania Creek study demonstrates, social action has a learning dimension and it makes political sense for activists to be attuned to it. Some of the most successful activists have treated social struggles as learning experiences (see, for example, Alinsky, 1971). It is also important for adult educators to understand that their formal educational work is but one part of a broad ensemble of education and learning. Educators who have grasped this are more sensitive and effective in their work (see, for example, Head, 1977).

Even a brief examination of the Terania Creek campaign demonstrates the *complex and contested* nature of social action and the informal learning associated with it. In the Terania Creek campaign activists learned about a host of matters, including rainforest science, the workings of bureaucracy and the political system, group dynamics, movement politics, the psychodynamics of individuals, strategic thinking, the mass media. This learning and action involved *struggle* – between conservationists and bureaucrats, forestry workers and business people – and among and within conservationists themselves. This theme – the complex and contested nature of informal social learning – will be developed further in the next chapter, which discusses women's experiences in two Australian community centres.

# CHAPTER 4

# The Neighbourhood House: Site of Struggle, Site of Learning

In Australia during the past twenty years there has been a significant growth of community-based social provision, in adult education and in other fields. A pattern has emerged of a local group expressing a desire for a particular service (e.g. health, childcare) or course, and a government-funded, often community-based, agency funding it (Johnson and Hinton, 1986: 13). Such demand often grows out of social activity. In suburbs and in country towns, it is common for women to begin meeting socially, and then to attempt to do something about issues that concern them – such as the need for childcare, or for transport, shops, community centres or adult education. Some of the positive aspects of the women's education that this development has given rise to have been discussed elsewhere (Benson and Saleeba, 1984; Kimberley, 1986; Clarke, 1987; Foley, 1991c; Savage, 1991). This chapter will look more closely at the dynamics of community-based adult learning, through an examination of informal learning in two neighbourhood centres in an Australian city. As in the previous two chapters, the various forms of learning that emerged in the houses will be described in some detail. But I will also attempt to develop a fuller explanation of the informal learning that emerged in the centres.

## Contestation and critical learning

A central contention of this book is that in order to understand informal and incidental learning in social action and sites we need to develop analyses which take account of specific social contexts, and which treat all aspects of adult learning as socially constructed and problematic. This requires both a broader notion of context and more detailed, specific analyses than are usually found in adult education theory. This chapter will attempt to place some signposts to such analyses, by applying concepts drawn from critical theory to data on informal and incidental learning in two neighbourhood centres.

The core concepts in this analysis will be *contestation, informal learning* and *critical learning*. As Terry Eagleton (1989: 167) has observed, human history can be interpreted as being characterised by domination, by 'the mind-shaking reality of consistent, unending, unruptured oppression and exploitation'. Feudalism, capitalism, state socialism – all have been systems of domination. This domination has had both a material and an ideological dimension. Domination originates in, and is constructed in, relationships of production and power, but it is also constructed in ideologies and discourses, that is in the ways in which people make meaning of situations and speak about them. So domination comes to be internalised, to be embedded in people's consciousness. (Giroux, 1984: 309–12; Kemmis and Fitzclarence, 1986: 96–98; Austin-Broos, 1987: 149–59; Patton, 1987: 228–33; Ball, 1990: 2). (This is to radically simplify a complex argument, and to gloss over the hotly contested issue of the determination of domination. For aspects of the domination debate, see Williams, 1973; Carr and Kemmis, 1986; Lears, 1985; Skinner, 1985; Metcalfe, 1988; Harvey, 1989; Ball, 1990; Game, 1991; Milner, 1991; Shilling, 1992).[1]

But if domination is universal, it is also continually contested, so history may also be seen as a continual struggle by ordinary people to maintain or extend control over their lives, through a process which, as we saw in Chapter 2, Gramsci (1971) named 'hegemonic struggle'. There is now a huge literature on this struggle for autonomy and liberation, ranging from E. P. Thompson's sweeping history of the English working class, to ethnographic studies of struggles for control in individual workplaces and classrooms (e.g. Anyon, 1983; Webb, 1990; Skeggs, 1991). The story of this struggle is one of gains and losses, of progress and retreat, and of a growing recognition of the *continually contested, complex, ambiguous*, and *contradictory* nature of the struggle between domination and liberation. While these concepts can be read into existing accounts of radical adult education projects (for example, the work of Myles Horton (see Adams, 1975) and Jane Thompson (1980, 1983)), the contestation problematic (see

Anyon, 1983; Walker and Barton, 1983; Wexler, 1987; Shilling, 1992) has been virtually ignored in adult education research. This neglect is part of a wider problem in adult education scholarship: its tendency to instrumentalism, psychological humanism, abstraction and idealism, and a general underdevelopment of sociological analysis.

A basic assumption of the contestation problematic is that contradiction and conflict are embedded in social life. As Walker and Barton (1983: 14) have noted, 'all social life involves a central contradictory principle in the sense that a person's individuality is both realised and restricted through participation in group life'. Within capitalist modes of production, fundamental contradictions operate in all spheres of social life: in production, in institutional life, and in cultural practices. As Barton and Walker point out, capitalist cultural practices, including learning and education, are contradictory in that they both reproduce 'attitudes, activities and artefacts which support ... the social order' and also 'produce recognitions, reactions and responses which provide for the development of a challenging and critical stance towards that order' (1983: 15).

The analytical difficulty is in separating the warp and the weft of reproduction and recognition. Here case studies which focus on the learning dimension of social life can be useful. Analysis of the dynamics of informal learning in different sites can produce insights into the way people develop critical consciousness, that is an understanding of themselves as social actors in struggles for autonomy and liberation. It is important to reiterate that these struggles are not 'sequential or logical' (Adams, 1975: 227), but are complex and contradictory. But by setting narratives of people's experiences alongside conditions for the development of critical consciousness, judgements can be made about whether or not instances of collective action are examples of critical learning.

In a paper on consciousness-raising groups in the women's movement, Hart (1990a: 48, 58) notes that in such work content (analysis of women's oppression), process (based on equality and reciprocity) and epistemology (starting from women's subjective experience) interweave and mutually determine one another. By working from women's experience, consciousness-raising groups are able to generate 'a particularly dense matrix of themes and questions directly relating to female oppression'. Hart argues that consciousness-raising work is emancipatory, focusing as it does on 'the internal and external effects of power' on women, and involving a process of critical reflection leading to a transformation of 'meaning perspectives' (Hart, 1990a: 48, 53). Warning that consciousness-raising can easily be coopted or distorted in educational settings, Hart sets out a number of 'enabling conditions' or principles for authentic consciousness-raising work. While Hart is writing about the intentional development of critical consciousness in women's groups, her principles provide a means of understanding the dynamics of critical and emancipatory informal learning in settings like neighbourhood centres.

Hart's five principles are:

1. The learning group must be representative of an oppressed or marginalised group.
2. The experience, assumptions and social position of members of the learning group must be relatively similar.
3. The learning group must develop a 'structure of equality'.
4. The members of the learning group must have the motivation and the time to reflect critically on their subjective experience.
5. Members of the learning group must gain a 'theoretical distance to personal experience'.

The fourth and fifth conditions require elaboration. As Freire notes, people are distinguished from other animals by their capacity for both action and reflection. People are 'capable of simultaneously transforming the world by their action and grasping and expressing the world's reality in creative language'. Their ability to reflect on their actions means people are potentially capable of emancipating themselves from oppressive social relationships: 'Only beings who can reflect upon the fact they are determined are capable of freeing themselves' (Freire, 1972a: 51–2. For more on the importance of reflection in learning, see Boud et al., 1985; and Boud and Walker, 1991). But, as Hart (1990a: 66–7) points out, to reflect *critically*, that is to understand the ways in which our consciousness is shaped by social relations and ideologies, requires 'the special powers of theory'. Theory 'does not follow the contours of immediate experience'. It 'sets a distance' which enables people 'to fathom aspects of the world hidden from the eyes of its own authors and actors', and to 'make transparent the relations that obtain among isolated and fragmented incidents of personal experience' (ibid.). This is the creative paradox of consciousness-raising work: personal experience is its necessary point of departure, but for critical consciousness to emerge people must gain theoretical distance from their subjective experience.

In this chapter I will argue that:

- the neighbourhood centres studied can be seen as 'sites of learning', arenas in which significant informal learning occurs, including the development of 'theoretical distance' and other elements of critical consciousness;
- this learning is frequently tacit or implicit, embedded as it is in the routine activities of women in the centres;
- much of this learning takes place in conflict, and these conflicts are shaped by individual, interpersonal, institutional and broader social and cultural factors;
- this informal learning is not automatic or inevitable.

## The houses

In their current form, neighbourhood centres (or 'houses' as they are locally known, after the ordinary houses in which they are generally located) emerged in Australia in the 1970s, their numbers increasing substantially in the 1980s. The houses were established for a variety of reasons: women's desire to come together to end their suburban isolation and obtain social and intellectual stimulation, to establish playgroups for young children, to provide education for women, to furnish productive outlets for women's skills. Typically, the original reason for participation led to other activities, in particular to the establishment of adult education classes for the women themselves, to some women participating in the management of neighbourhood houses, and, in some cases, to women working in the houses as voluntary or paid workers (Gravell and Nelson, 1986).

The houses that will be discussed here are both in the same city, one in Higby,[2] an inner-city suburb, the other in Sage, an outer suburb. Higby Neighbourhood House started in the late 1970s as a drop-in centre for women and a playgroup location. It is now a registered cooperative with membership open to all interested residents. Higby is administered by an elected committee of seven and is located in a house owned by the local council. Higby is rare among neighbourhood houses in that a large proportion of its budget is federally – funded and because it did not have to struggle for funds until the early 1990s. Sage Neighbourhood House was established in the early 1980s and targets disadvantaged women. It has a large volunteer and paid staff. All local residents can become members of the centre, which has a committee of management of twelve. The centre hosts a range of activities, projects and facilities, including adult education classes, playgroups, a consumer and tenancy programme, community development and environment projects, and discussion and self-help groups.

## Methodology

The original intention of the research on which this chapter is based was to examine women's studies courses in neighbourhood houses, a theme discussed briefly in an earlier paper (Foley, 1991c). An initial taped discussion in April 1991 with ten members of one of the houses pointed to the importance of both informal learning and learning in conflict in the houses. Further individual and group interviews on these themes were conducted in April and October 1991, and in April–May 1992. Interviews were open-ended, but were intended to unearth narratives which would facilitate an understanding of the learning dimension of interviewees' experience of the houses. After each of the three rounds of interviews a draft paper was distributed to the interviewees. A seminar of fifty people concerned with neighbourhood houses discussed a second draft of the paper.

## Learning in the houses

1. *Finding a place* When asked why they became involved in a house, some women spoke of a sharply felt need to end their isolation. Trish, whose involvement in the house led to her becoming a community worker, brought two daughters to the Sage playgroup but subsequently lost contact with the house. Then one of her close friends went back to work:

> It wasn't until she did that I realised how much of a companion she'd been. ... I felt lost, really lonely, and went through a whole self-analysis thing where you think 'What am I doing? Who am I?' and felt the whole thing of being a Mum and not a Trish, if you can understand that. You tend to lose yourself, you become somebody else's person. I figured I had

to get out of it, I had to do something about it. So I decided to join the committee of management here.

Participation in playgroups helped women to recognise their common interests, and to end their suburban isolation. Rita, a member of Higby House, recalls:

I learnt that there were a lot of other people in the same situation as I was. When I finished work I didn't know anyone else in Higby. I'd been living here for three years ... and didn't know any of the facilities available. I learnt where to go, where to look for things, how to find out what was available, and met lots of different women. Right from the word go, because I started going out when my daughter was so young, I never felt stuck at home and trapped, and I knew places to go. To get out, and not to be stuck at home climbing the walls. So many people get to that stage and then find this place. I think I was lucky that I found it very early.

Soon after Sage House was established, Doreen, then in her early twenties, was persuaded by one of the Sage workers to take on a part-time child-minding job in the house. After four years of this, Doreen left the house to take up a job in a local supermarket. 'I wanted to expand myself, and I felt that being a childcare worker I couldn't do that. I needed to get out and meet more people, and I was always in here and I couldn't.' During the same period she left her husband, who was becoming progressively more abusive and violent. Doreen left the area for some years, returning towards the end of 1990.

When I came back I had a lot of problems, but everyone here has been supportive. ... They were all pleased to see that I had accomplished what I wanted to do, and sort of begun my life again. ... [It's] taken a lot of years to get back on track again, ... going through separation, divorce, abuse, stuff like that. But the Centre's always been here for me, to sort of help me get through it. Coming here I always know there's a friendly ear ...

One gets a sense of the house as a safe, supportive place. But the houses are not always warm and welcoming: people sometimes have to struggle for a place. At Higby, where 40 per cent of the students in courses were migrant women, Conchita, an active member, herself an immigrant, explained the low participation of migrant women in the house's committee of management by referring to her own experience:

When I first came here ... I could see all these people having a normal conversation at the [kitchen] table. It was so overwhelming, I was just sitting in one corner. I liked to be there but at the same time felt very uncomfortable because my level of English wasn't the same as theirs. ... Perhaps if I'd been more outgoing. ... I couldn't follow a lot of their conversation and they didn't notice it. ... I could talk one to one, or with a group of children, but not [with] a group of adults. It was very confusing. I remember that after a week in the house I was in a very bad mood at home, saying, 'What am I doing here?' But I decided to stay and see what happened and it was really good, and I got a lot from this house ...

2. *Learning through participation*   Once they attend playgroups with their children, many women undergo a gradual and sometimes confused and painful process of asking for something for themselves. This something might be any or all of involvement in education or other house activities, participation in the management of a house, or paid or voluntary work in a house or elsewhere. Explicit women's education in neighbourhood houses is significant in both process and outcomes, and has been discussed elsewhere (see Kimberley, 1986; Clarke, 1987; Foley, 1991c; Savage, 1991). But the whole experience of participating in a house is an important learning process for women. Much of this learning is informal and incidental, it is embedded in other activities, and it is often not articulated as learning by neighbourhood house members.

At Sage, a discussion with four working-class women revealed a common experience of expanded knowledge and growing self-confidence as a result of participation in the house. Initially, the women approached the house cautiously. When Heidi first came to the house 'it was very frightening, very sort of, don't know what to expect. But after a while you get used to it.' She began by getting involved in the house's multi-cultural women's group. In this group, which met fortnightly, women from non-English-speaking backgrounds 'just got a cup of tea and a chat, sometimes we'd do craft, sometimes we'd have guest speakers, outings'. After some time a house worker asked Heidi if she would 'like to do a couple of hours voluntary work, just answering the phone and general inquiries'. Five years later Heidi had been consistently involved in the house, both as a volunteer and through holding several short-term paid positions in the house, 'computer work, typing, things like that'.

Looking back on her experience, Heidi considered she had learned a lot:

> Half the things I've learnt here I would never have known if I would have stayed at home. … Things on domestic violence. How to get intervention orders, what to do, how to protect yourself and things like that. The same with, we've got a consumer worker here. … If something [I bought] was faulty, I might have gone back and said, 'Oh look, this is no good.' They might say, 'You've used it already? Yeah? Sorry, we can't give it back.' And I would have gone, that would have been it. But apparently now you can go to the consumer [affairs regulatory agency] here, ask them, they'll help you, they'll tell you what you can do. There's so many things. There's not a day goes by when you don't learn something new. It's sort of an education, isn't it?

That the knowledge is acquired informally is made clear by another comment of Heidi's:

> It's funny you know, you try not to listen to people when they're having a conversation on the phone (laughs). But you're down this end, you've got an ear this way, and it's so informal, unless it's really something hush hush …

One of the most frequently mentioned outcomes of participation in the houses is a growth in, or a regaining of, self-esteem and self-confidence. Specifically, the women come to see themselves, and to be seen, as competent people with something to contribute to society beyond their roles as mothers.

> *Heidi*: When it comes time to write your resumé, when you put down you can do this, this and this, you think: Look at all the things I've done. … You think: Crikies, can I do all this?

> *Doreen*: I find that Nikki, my eldest, she looks up to me because I'm out there trying to do something, to make something of myself. So she encourages it, you know.

> *Antonia, a volunteer grief counsellor at Sage*: The … confidence that you had before comes back, because it died down a little bit staying at home for a while. … You're just a housewife. People think, 'She's got nothing to talk about, so let's not talk to her'. … It does connect you, doesn't it, back to your kids again. Because as they grow up they think you're just a Mum. And now all of a sudden you're relating with a lot of different areas that they come across in their life. … What happens is I take [things that happen in the neighbourhood house] home, and they realise that

there is a world that I'm involved in now, and they want to know what's
happening in my world ...

3. *Learning through conflict* Conflict and struggle are central to informal learning in neighbourhood houses, something that was expressed very clearly by one of the women interviewed:

> This place as much as anything is about conflict – really difficult stuff
> about learning, the difficulty of getting people on committees, the diffi-
> culty of getting people to work together. ... Intense friendships are made
> and then broken, lots of difficult things happen here ...

In Higby House, struggles over childcare have been at the heart of
this process of informal learning. The initial reason for the house's
existence was a children's playgroup. But quite soon 'a kind of education by stealth' emerged in response to learning needs expressed by
women attending the playgroup. A class was set up to teach women
to drive. Turkish and Arabic women's groups were established, initially
with a social focus, but the women soon started having English
lessons. An Italian-speaking childcare worker conducted a bilingual
playgroup and that also led to Italian lessons for the English-speaking
members of the group. These and other activities, such as a netball
team and committee of management meetings (which 'were always
chaos because the kids were there'), raised the need for childcare.

But the women found it difficult to demand childcare. 'There was
this real prejudice in those days [the early 1980s] about childcare.'
There was a 'sense that it was valid to have childcare if you were
earning an income', but 'if by choice you were at home being a
mother it was different'. Most of the 'first generation' of house
members, the women who had established the house, felt guilty about
demanding something for themselves. The dominant feeling was 'I
don't really need this place for myself': it was a 'real playgroup
mentality, you had to be here with your kids, doing stuff with your
kids'. But the educational and other activities referred to above had
begun, and women needed to be freed from childcare responsibilities
so they could pursue those activities. Newer members of the house
suggested that people take turns in minding children on Friday morn-
ings. This suggestion was resisted by older members and 'a huge
debate ensued ... between the old guard and the newer people ...
and eventually the new guard won and the Friday morning roster

was established'. People still participated in playgroups on other days, but 'come Friday morning they came here, dropped their kids off, mostly with great delight, and went off' to do other things.

Women who participated in the struggle for childcare at Higby remember it as a decisive phase in the life of the house. The Friday morning roster became 'an enormously strong focus in the house'. 'The people who were really active in the house – the "movers", the "second generation" of house members – gravitated around' the roster. The roster helped to focus house activities: 'women now knew that their children would be minded while they went off to do other things'. The women who participated in the roster became a close, 'strong' and 'committed' group, 'a real support network'. In 1986, this group, through one of the house workers, secured funding from the local technical and further education college to enable the house to become a community provider of adult education. Starting with a women's discussion group, women's studies and tertiary bridging courses soon became central to the house's activities.

But if, in retrospect, participants can see how important the establishment of the Friday morning roster was in releasing house members' energies, they also remember the struggle for childcare as fierce and difficult, and one in which individuals learned political skills and clarified their political positions. Mary, the first worker employed in the house, remembers the conflict over childcare as 'the first big struggle, and the first big learning experience for me and other people'. While Mary admired the older members for their achievements in setting up the house, 'I was pretty clear about whose side I was on' in the childcare issue. 'Because it was to do with opening the place up, and making it accessible to more people and different people … ' Mary worked with the newer members to 'stack' a meeting of house members which was called to fill a vacancy on the house committee of management.

> I'd *never* done that before in my life, I was so frightened about it. … It put you in direct conflict with certain individuals, which was something I'd never had to do before, in my work life. … And there was all that thing about it being a women's place, and it's a community centre, and we're all girls together, and we're all working together on this. And there was that, but there was also the conflict there about, 'Alright, you're in this group of women here, with certain needs and ideas. There's this other group. And trying to make decisions about which way it should go … '.

Looking back, Mary believes she was going through a rather torturous process of 'coming to terms with and putting into action' what she really wanted, professionally and politically.

> ... [I]t was what I perceived as a worker was needed and wanted. It was also the sort of place I wanted to work in. I didn't want to work in a place with all these – I used to call them 'mothers who wanted to be mothers'. ... I thought, 'Well, if that's what they want, they can have playgroups in their lounge rooms, they don't need a community centre'. It was this whole thing of actually admitting to yourself, and then to others, 'This is what I value, and this is what I want'. And it works on a political level, and on a ... personal level. ... Because I was young and relatively unpoliticised and I wanted to 'help' the community, [I had] a very unformed approach to it, and it gradually had to harden up and get more focused in terms of what I was on about, in terms of my values and political leanings.

She sees the house members who came to demand childcare as having gone through a similar process:

> Also for the people who came there to use or take part in the place: 'I come here for my children, because I'm a good mother and this was a good thing to do with the children.' And gradually it becomes obvious that you are also there for yourself. And as you join in the activities, or the running of the house, or the learning activities, you have to come to terms with: 'This is what I want, as well as being a mother.' But it's hard, because of the sort of pressure on people, especially first time around parents, this is the be-all and end-all ...

4. *Critical learning*   In the State in which the neighbourhood houses exist, community organisations wishing to gain access to government funds are required to become incorporated organisations administered by committees of management. Committees are elected annually by the organisations' members and are responsible for policy, finance and staffing. In neighbourhood houses members frequently move from involvement in playgroups to participation in the committee.

Women interviewed felt they had learned a lot through being committee members. They learned about how the house operated, how to read and keep accounts, how to make collective decisions and how to plan and budget. They also developed a clearer understanding of broader women's issues: 'the lack of resources and facilities' for women, for example. Most importantly, perhaps, participation in the committees gave women experience of the complexities of trying to run organisations in democratic, 'women-centred' ways .

The committees, like other aspects of the life of the houses, were sites of struggle as well as learning. Interviewees constantly referred to both the importance and the difficulties of trying to develop a non-hierarchical way of administering the houses. At Higby House in the late 1980s the Friday morning roster collapsed because eight of the twelve women who participated in it had second babies at around the same time. This was followed by another 'generational change' as the active members' children grew up and the activists left the house and became involved in other activities.

The next generation of house members used the house differently from the preceding generation, largely, it appears, because of the economic malaise of the late 1980s and early 1990s. Many of the women who now used the house, had, or wanted, part-time jobs and were interested in courses that would lead to work or further education. The Higby committee was 'virtually non-existent' from the end of 1990, and in April 1991 had only three members. At the previous annual general meeting 'four or five' committee members had resigned 'because of friction with staff'. In 1991 conflict between members and staff continued. In interviews with house members this conflict was initially attributed to 'personality clashes – the coop members being a bit picky with staff, and staff members being very defensive'. But later the interviewees suggested that the source of the conflict lay in the lack of clear house policies and guidelines for workers, and in poor communication between committee members and workers. This was a theme that was echoed in interviews with an earlier generation of house members.

There was also a strong feeling that differences between committee and staff had a structural basis. Rhona, a former committee member, saw the problem as partly lying in differences in the positions and power of committee members and workers:

> The power-base of the committee of management is uncertain. The committee is technically the employer, but the employees have more ongoing knowledge of the affairs of the House. The tenure of staff is usually much longer than that of the committee, but staff are subject to constant revision of the rules of their employment, while possessing much of the acquired knowledge about the House. ... The experience of Higby House has been of repeated bouts of conflict between staff

(established with knowledge/power) and changing committees (unsure of their knowledge and power, reluctant to accept old rules which may no longer be appropriate, but tentative about creating new rules) ...

Rhona saw the source of the structural problem as being the house's relationship with the State, and recognised that there was no ready solution to the problem:

Higby Neighbourhood House has to be an incorporated body to receive funding. ... Fundamentally, the employment/control model imposed by the funding body is inappropriate. It exacerbates the conflict involved when women are struggling to create more democratic and sensitive ways of relating to one another and running organisations.

This contradiction was felt by the women very sharply. Rhona remembered how uncomfortable she felt when, as a committee member, she had to tell workers who had pointed out to the committee that they were being paid under-award wages 'we don't have the money to pay you. ... It's fine for us to recognise what you deserve, but if our funding is finite we can bake ten thousand cakes and we're still not going to make enough money to pay your top-up wages.'

Mary, who was a worker at Higby at the same time that Rhona was a committee member, also remembered salary negotiations as difficult and painful, partly because of her own resistance to acquiring information about industrial issues, but also because of the difficulty committee members experienced in 'actually performing their employer responsibilities'. Mary recalled that the committee members 'did things on a personal level to try to compensate for' workers low wages:

There was a Christmas bonus of a half-case of champagne. ... When each staff member left [there was] the most fantastic going-away party, that sort of thing. ... So, on the one hand, you've got these people who do all these wonderful things for you ... cook you beautiful meals when you go round to their place, all that personal way of saying, 'You're terrific, you're doing a great job, we appreciate what you're doing' ...

On the other hand, Mary came to think, the warmth with which the committee treated workers was a way of 'avoiding the realities of being an employer'. Workers also got caught up in this avoidance, which was exacerbated by the existence in the house of an ideology that maintained that 'this employment situation transcends all that,

that's all nasty stuff that only goes on in adversarial employment situations'.

Mary was 'gradually becoming aware of it as a problem, but I very much saw it as *my* fault, because I couldn't assert myself. ... But it was just an impossible position to be in, educating your employer to be a good employer.' The conflict over worker wages was 'disillusioning' and 'upsetting' for workers. These feelings were heightened by the way the older group of house activists, 'who were terrific, who we'd relied on, and who we'd come very close to personally', were treating newer members. 'It was awful to see. ... Excluding people from decision-making processes, not in an overt way, the way you can run meetings just to keep new people out ... '.

The staff finally wrote a grievance paper, and put it to a committee meeting. The committee was 'furious': 'that meeting just disintegrated, nothing much came out of it'. But it was followed by other meetings, and informal discussions: 'people asking you around to tea and asking you, "What's wrong, why are you being like this?"'. This in turn led to a workshop with an external facilitator who

> tried to help people come out and say what they really meant, instead of skirting around the edges. That was quite useful. Though people were still really hurt, it put it back in perspective a bit, and more attempts were made to at least formally make sure that there was a process by which newer people could be included and encouraged on to committees. But I think a lot of people had lost heart [and withdrew from the house]. It was time for them to do that anyway, their kids were getting older ...

Rhona recalls the intervention of Mary and her fellow workers as having had a beneficial effect on the functioning of the committee.

> People like Mary, by forcing these issues, were really forcing people who were on committee to have to find new information, to have to take employment responsibilities that involved a lot of learning for them [but] that they were really reluctant to have to pursue. It was now, 'Who's going to do this?' at committee meetings, and there'd be a deadly silence all the time because nobody wanted to do it, because nobody had the industrial experience. And so it was forcing people who were on committee to go out and pick up those jobs.

Eventually the committee pursued, and after a long struggle obtained, other sources of funds to supplement the workers' wages. This search in turn generated learning about the grudging and tentative nature of the State's commitment to the funding of community agencies, and about the practicalities of garnering funds from a variety of sources. When the Higby committee pointed out to its funding body, a Federal Government department, that its grant did not enable the house to pay its workers award wages, the department redefined itself as the house's 'principal' rather than its sole funding body, and told the committee to look for other sources of funds. Rhona recalls that the Higby committee felt that to be treated in this way by the State bureaucracy, under a Labor Government, was a 'contradiction' and an 'ideological dilemma'. It was also 'a practical dilemma': 'where on earth to find the money it they weren't going to give it to us'.

## Conclusions

On the basis of the data reviewed here, only the first of Hart's five conditions for the existence of authentic consciousness-raising work is unequivocally met in the neighbourhood houses. There is insufficient evidence to make judgements about the extent to which the second and third conditions are met in the houses. But, for the purposes of this book, it is the fourth and fifth conditions that are of greatest interest. There is some sign in the houses of the emergence of critical consciousness and its precondition, theoretical distance. In considering the following conclusions, two points should be kept in mind. First, the small amount of data examined in this case study only allow an identification of apparent tendencies, clues to be tested by further research. Secondly, the identification of the emergence of critical consciousness is difficult, because its growth is both complex and fragile. As Skeggs has pointed out, change in consciousness

> is not marked by a simple progression from one position of subjectivity to another. Rather it is characterised by an oscillation between moments of relative incoherence, the breaking up of old political languages and positions, and moments when new formulations, often tentative and transitory, are being realised. (Skeggs, 1991: 136)

What, then, can be concluded about the nature of informal learning in the neighbourhood houses? First, the women's reflections on their experiences and learnings in the houses show that they were wrestling with what Barton and Walker see as the central contradiction of social life, the way in which 'a person's individuality is both realised and restricted through participation in group life'. There is often an implicit recognition of this dilemma in the women's reflections. Recalling the experience of women in childcare groups at Higby, Mary felt that

> trying to function ... in a more communal way was quite difficult. ... You got lots of support, there were lots of people, you could ask for help, just social contact. But also when you're dealing with a group of ten or twelve or fifteen kids, the kids fight, they bite each other, people get really embarrassed about how their kids behave, there's competition ..., people compare [their children]. ... Sometimes it was handled really well, and people were supported through times of low confidence. ... And other times it wasn't handled well, and people were made to feel worse ... and weren't properly supported. I mean, it wasn't magic. Just because it was a group of fairly committed people together, who basically wanted the same things, it didn't make the nasty things go away. I think there was plenty of hurt inflicted along the way, unfortunately.

Secondly, the data reported here suggest that neighbourhood houses can be seen as 'liberated spaces' in which women have opportunities to explore their experience and build women-centred, nurturing relationships. The houses can also be viewed as 'sites of learning'. In the houses, women learn in playgroups, in courses, through their participation in committees of management, and in their roles as community workers. Through participating in house activities, women gain instrumental skills and knowledge, as well as self-awareness and an understanding of the complexity of interpersonal relationships. They also become clearer about their own values and they recognise that, because people have different interests and values, conflict among them is inevitable, and that the conflict can be constructive or destructive. The women also learn that wider contextual and structural factors shape what happens in the houses. Much of this learning is informal, incidental and embedded in other activities. It is often not articulated as learning by the people who do it, but it is still very significant learning.

The houses can also be seen as sites of struggle, and the struggles themselves as providing opportunities for learning. These struggles might be with one's self, against one's own sex-role socialisation. So, for example, the women at Higby had to overcome their belief that housework was not work before they could demand childcare in the house and free themselves to pursue non-playgroup activities. Life in the houses also generates struggles between individuals and groups. So, at Higby, there was a decisive debate over childcare between older and newer members, and there was a difficult and painful struggle over workers' wages. Such struggles have the potential to be destructive and debilitating. But they can also lead to decisive, liberating, action, which itself is full of learning for the people involved. For example, the early struggle over childcare at Higby freed the women involved to pursue other activities. This struggle also helped to create a close, strong, committed group of house members, 'a real support network'.

Although struggles within neighbourhood houses are often painful for the individuals involved, and although they can and do lead into cul-de-sacs of destructive conflict, they also generate what is probably the most significant sort of human learning. This is learning that enables people to make sense of, and act on, their environment, and to come to understand themselves as knowledge-creating, acting beings. Through their participation in neighbourhood houses, women have learned to overcome the fear and lack of confidence instilled in them by their gender socialisation, to fight for something for themselves and to participate in difficult collective decision-making. They have also developed an understanding of the individual and social sources of conflict, a capacity to analyse situations contextually and act on them strategically, and an ability to examine and act on their own values and goals. All this is clearly *critical* learning: it involves the deprivatisation of previously apparently idiosyncratic experience, the completion of understandings, the opening up of possibilities for action, and changes in 'the structure and the frame of experience' (Hart, 1990a: 55). This process of critical learning involves people in theorising their experience: they stand back from it and reorder it, using concepts like power, conflict, structure, values and choice. It is also clear that this critical learning is gained informally, through experience, by acting and reflecting on action, rather than in formal courses.

This said, it is important to re-emphasise the complexities, ambiguities and contradictions of life and learning in neighbourhood houses. For example, voluntary work in the houses, valuable as it might be for individual women, opens up a further unpaid, unaccredited arena of exploitation of female labour.[3] Again, informal learning in the houses frequently appears to be latent and is not recognised by learners *as* learning. At this stage the processes by which experience becomes learning (see Boud et al., 1985; Boud and Walker, 1991) are not clearly understood. Much more remains to be discovered about the characteristics, determinants, dynamics and effects of informal, embedded learning in community centres and other social sites. We also need to develop a fuller understanding of the ways in which informal and incidental learning are shaped by broader social forces. This is the subject of the next three chapters.

## Notes

1. In saying this, I am taking a clearly materialist position on complex debates about determination and domination within historical materialism and critical theory. For aspects of these debates, see Williams, 1973; Lears, 1985; Skinner, 1985; Carr and Kemmis, 1986; Kemmis and Fitzclarence, 1986; Wood, 1986; Metcalfe, 1988; Harvey, 1989; Ball, 1990; Milner, 1991; Shilling, 1992.

2. The houses, and their members, have been given fictitious names.

3. I am indebted to Anita Devos for this point.

# CHAPTER 5

# Adult Education and Capitalist Reorganisation

In the introduction to this book I suggested that satisfactory accounts of learning in struggle make connections between learning and education and four other variables – political economy, micro-politics, ideology and discourse. In Chapters 2–4 I focused on the dynamics of learning in local struggles. My intention was to portray the complex and at times contradictory ways that people learn in social action and community organisations. I located these case studies in their broader economic and political contexts, but only in the sketchiest of ways. In this chapter and the next two I pay closer attention to the broader (or 'macro')-political and economic determinants of local struggles and learning. I argue that an understanding of the varied and changing ways in which the political economy of capitalism plays itself out in particular situations is central to a strong account of learning in struggle. This chapter offers an extended analysis of the political economy of economic and workplace restructuring in the current period. I argue that such an analysis not only generates a clearer understanding of changes in educational policy and practice, it also brings to light a generally unrecognised but highly important form of workplace learning, workers' resistant learning.

## 'Restructuring', or 'capitalist reorganisation'?

I will argue in this chapter that historical materialist analysis, developed in relation to specific social situations, is essential to any attempt to connect radical adult education to people's lives and struggles. Starting with the much used (and abused) notion of 'economic restructuring', and examining it particularly in relation to the last decade in Australia, I will argue that

1. The received notion of economic 'restructuring' is a myth which masks the actual processes of capitalist reorganisation. The current phase of capitalist reorganisation has been misinterpreted by policy-makers, and some adult educators, who are promoting simplistic technical 'solutions' to complex social problems.
2. To understand 'restructuring' it is essential to understand capitalism. Capitalism is an inherently unstable system, involving constant growth, continual exploitation of labour, constant technological change, and periodic crises. Capitalism is also a system of economic, political and cultural domination, which is continually contested by those it exploits.
3. Adult education, through its instrumentalist, professionalised and decontextualised practices and discourses, is implicated in processes of capitalist domination and capitalist reorganisation. Adult educators who wish to contribute to struggles against capitalist domination must stop seeing adult learning and education as purely technical, interpersonal and institutionalised activities. They must recognise that adult education and learning are also complex, and contested, social, cultural and historical processes. Above all, they must learn to recognise and work with workers' resistant learning.

## Myths of restructuring

The conventional wisdom is that we are living in a post-Fordist, post-modernist, post-socialist and, some would argue, post-industrial, age. The essential elements of this thesis are:

1. A system of mass production and consumption, called 'Fordism' after the founder of assembly-line production, and also known as 'welfare capitalism', was dominant in western industrialised countries, including Australia, from the 1920s to the 1970s. In these years Fordism delivered economic growth, high wages, high levels of consumption, and social security to the majority of people in those countries.
2. Since the 1970s, Fordism has been in crisis, for a variety of reasons, including: saturation of consumer markets in the developed countries; the emergence of mass production in cheaper labour areas,

and the consequent 'de-industrialisation' of western economies; the collapse of the Bretton Woods financial system in the 1970s; the emergence of 'stagflation' (simultaneous inflation and economic stagnation).

3. The general response to the crisis in Fordism has been for countries to try to stimulate export production by reducing government expenditure, reducing real wages, providing incentives for private investment, production and consumption, devaluing currencies, reducing government regulation of business activity and encouraging foreign investment. While conservatives have sought to break the power of organised labour, and social democrats have adopted a more consensual approach to industrial relations, western governments have all aimed to create technologically advanced, low labour-cost, export-oriented, internationally competitive economies.

4. There has been remarkably little dissent from this policy prescription. Even among socialists the choice has usually been posed as being between an intensified Fordism, (i.e. mass production intensified by computer technology), and 'flexible specialisation', involving technologically sophisticated production by skilled workers for niche markets. In the flexible specialisation scenario, it is maintained that the contradictions of Fordism have led to its demise and its replacement by production that is once more controlled by the producers, albeit a much smaller group, an elite of technician-managers. The argument is that western countries have no real choice: they either take the flexible specialisation path or they face continuing de-industrialisation, declining living standards, and economic vulnerability – they become, in the words of the former Australian Prime Minister, Paul Keating, 'banana republics'. (For discussion of Fordism and the post-Fordist thesis, see Harvey, 1989: 121–97; Mathews, 1989a and 1989b; Devos, 1991; Hampson, 1991; Hyman, 1991; Pollert, 1991.)

5. In the post-Fordist problematic, education is to contribute to flexible specialisation by focusing on vocational training. Education systems, it is argued, should concentrate on developing people's competencies – their skills, knowledge and values – to enable them to move across jobs, from one sector of the economy to the other, and even from one country to another. Curricula should be redesigned along competency-based lines, enabling the recognition

of existing competence, as well as the more effective articulation of different levels of education and training. Education is seen as one component of a comprehensive approach to workplace restructuring, one which includes changes in industrial relations, technology and workplace organisation. The aim is a highly skilled, mobile workforce which will help to make industry internationally competitive. (For an Australian exposition of this thesis, see Gonczi, 1992: 9–78.)

The post-Fordist problematic has invented a mythical world of lean, mean, technologically advanced, growth economies competing with one another in a perfect global market. The flexibility thesis rests on flawed assumptions. One does not have to be an economist to work out that (a) the 'market' is not 'perfect', that it is, in fact, controlled by a small number of countries and corporations, with disastrous results for the majority of the world's people; (b) even if the competition was fair, not every country could win; and (c) in an age of environmental collapse, to advocate economic growth in the 'developed' countries is breathtakingly irresponsible. It is equally clear that adult education and learning are not mere technical processes in a neutral process of economic restructuring.

An examination of the literature reveals significant problems with the post-Fordist thesis. First, 'Fordism' was neither a monolithic regime of mass production, nor a golden age of full employment and social welfare. Production for small and specialised markets has long existed in industrialised countries; even in the car industry there have been segmented markets for at least fifty years. The prosperity of the 'welfare state' was built on a segmented workforce, and particularly on the super-exploited labour of women, ethnic groups and immigrants (Hyman, 1991: 266–7; Pollert, 1991). Secondly, the flexible specialisation theorists focus on manufacturing industry, on technological change, and on markets, and pay little attention to the role of capital, state and social struggle in economic and workplace change (Hyman, 1991: 266). Post-Fordist explanations therefore give a partial and distorted account of economic and workplace change.

By focusing on the alleged emergence of the 'autonomous' skilled worker in manufacturing industry, the flexible specialisation problematic directs our attention away from the bulk of the workforce. In the expanding services sector of the economy, which is already much larger than the manufacturing sector, much labour is poorly paid, untrained, routinised and insecure. It appears that already-existing labour market segmentation is intensifying. There is a proportionally small primary or core labour market of managers, professionals, technicians and skilled workers whose skills and/or qualifications secure them lifetime employment. There is a much larger secondary or peripheral workforce who are in sporadic and grossly exploited employment, and who at any time can be relegated to a third group which is variously described as the unemployed, the marginalised or the underclass. Terms like the 'two-thirds/one-third society', the 'third-worldisation' of advanced industrial countries, and the 'South Africanisation of society' are used to describe this intensified segmentation. It is also noted that the 'servile class', the super-exploited workers who service the consumption needs of capital and the primary workforce are predominantly female, ethnic, immigrant and people of the 'third world' (Hyman, 1991: 267–8, 271–2).

The flexible specialisation thesis even misrepresents the position of core workers in the production process. As Hyman and others have noted, the introduction of 'flexible' micro-electronic technology does not inevitably lead to workers being more involved in their work. These writers note the ongoing tension in capitalist production between management's desire to control the work process and the need for workers to exercise intelligence and initiative in work. The introduction of new technology, rather than resolving this tension, generates new permutations of it. Responses to the emergence of micro-electronic technology have ranged from attempts to introduce it without changing existing management/worker relationships, to linking its introduction to the development of semi-autonomous work groups, to attempts to incorporate new technology in a broader strategy of weakening workers' collective influence in the workplace (Hyman, 1991: 269–71).

The fundamental flaw in the post-Fordist model is that it presents economic and workplace restructuring as technical rather than historical, political and ideological processes. Whatever the intention of its advocates, the post-Fordist/flexible specialisation thesis has to be seen as an ideological myth, masking the actual dynamics of the reorganisation of the global political economy. The goal of this reorganisation is capital's eternal goal: the extraction of more of the surplus of workers' labour, and the further accumulation of capital.

Capital's intention, as ever, is contested by those whom it seeks to exploit. In the rest of this chapter I hope to throw some light on this struggle over capitalist reorganisation, and on the role of adult learning and education in it.

## Domination and struggle in capitalism

To understand 'restructuring' we need to understand capitalism. In September 1992, in Brisbane, Australia, a group of textile workers jeered their own union secretary as she left the Industrial Relations Commission. The union had opposed an enterprise agreement between the workers and their employer. Under the agreement, which *The Australian* newspaper described as 'pace-setting', workers at the Gazal Clothing Company would have agreed to work part-time for up to five months of the year, and would have abandoned their right to holiday pay and sick pay. The union did not oppose these provisions. But it insisted that workers who resigned because they, in the words of the union secretary, 'could not afford to live on two days pay a week', received a proper severance package. The managing director of the company said (to directly quote *The Australian*) that 'he could not afford to make such a commitment as it could bankrupt the family-owned business'.

Several characteristics of contemporary capitalism are represented in this story. In a capitalist economy some people (capitalists) own and control the means of production and others (workers) sell their labour to the capitalists. Under this arrangement, workers produce goods and services which are sold in the market. Capitalists extract the surplus of workers' labour, that is the capitalist takes whatever profit remains after the costs of production (including labour costs) have been met. If capitalists cannot make a profit, or they see an opportunity to increase profits, they seek to reorganise (or restructure) production, usually by lowering the cost of labour and/or applying new technology. Workers both accommodate to and resist this process. Conflict – class struggle between labour and capital – is consequently endemic in capitalism. Government – more usefully termed the state[1] – seeks to channel conflict between labour and capital by establishing legal frameworks and mediating bodies. The state can also have a powerful effect on industrial relations by withdrawing from the industrial relations arena. This is currently occurring in Australia, with a shift from centralised wage negotiations through government-appointed arbitration bodies to a system of direct bargaining at the enterprise level. The advocates of these new arrangements argue that they are more democratic because they give workers the opportunity to deal directly with their employers, and the choice of belonging or not belonging to a trade union. The Gazal example illustrates how vulnerable workers can be in the new dispensation, and reveals the real agenda of the advocates of this version of enterprise bargaining: massive productivity increases through a radical reduction in labour costs.

The class struggle also has a cultural dimension. There are different ways of interpreting it, related to the position of actors in the struggle. In our example, *The Australian*'s article is written from the perspectives of the capitalist and the workers who wish to reach an agreement with him. This is not surprising, given that the newspaper is owned by a media baron (Rupert Murdoch) who is renowned for his hostility to trade unions and who has used police power to enforce enterprise agreements with his own workers. Finally, the Gazal example directs our attention to the role of capitalism's third class, the middle class. The journalist who wrote the article is a worker: he sells his labour in return for a wage. But he is a relatively privileged worker, in terms of the level of his wage, the security of his employment and the job mobility his professional qualification gives him. The chances are that he will identify with his employer rather than other workers. In this sense journalists and other middle-class workers frequently perform the function of a service class, furthering, however unconsciously, the interests of capital.

It is useful to note some other important features of the capitalist mode of production here. One is that economic growth is essential to capitalism, 'since it is only through growth that profits can be assured'. Capitalism has to grow, 'no matter what the social, political … or ecological consequences'. 'Crisis is then defined as lack of growth.' Three things follow from this. One is that as capitalist growth depends on the exploitation of labour, the control of labour is essential. Another is that 'capitalism is necessarily technologically and organisationally dynamic' . A third is that change and crisis are endemic in capitalism. In particular, the growth imperative of capitalism leads to periodic crises of *overaccumulation*, in which idle capital and idle labour coexist. (Harvey, 1989: 180) As we have seen, the world has been experiencing one such crisis since the early 1970s.

Historically, capitalism has dealt with crises of overaccumulation in three ways: through devaluation or destruction of productive capacity or the money value of commodities; through state planning and regulation; or through temporal and spatial displacement (Harvey, 1989: 181–4). The problem, for capital and for all of us, is that each attempt to deal with an overaccumulation crisis leads to further problems. For example, the post-World War Two boom rested on Keynesian macro-economic management and spatial displacements of capital (into the suburbs and the 'sunbelt' in the United States, into the reconstruction of the European and Japanese economies, and into the cheap labour areas of the third world). But these strategies created their own problems. Keynesian debt-financing created mountains of debt which many countries are still trying to deal with. Government attempts to monetise away this debt led to inflation. Third world industry undercut first world manufacturing, leading to de-industrialisation and chronic unemployment in developed countries (Harvey, 1989: 184–7).

In this analysis, 'post-Fordism' is seen to be not the answer to global economic problems but a temporary and partial solution to the inherent instability of capitalism. Given the nature of capitalism, the post-Fordist strategy must itself create further problems, which different interest groups will struggle over and societies will have to try to deal with. As Harvey shows so clearly, although there has been a significant reorganisation of capitalism over the past twenty years, 'the underlying logic of capitalist accumulation and its crisis tendencies remain the same' (Harvey, 1989: 189). At its core, capitalism is a system of 'creative destruction', involving constant growth, continual exploitation of labour and constant technological change. It is also a system of economic, political and cultural domination, which is continually contested by ordinary people.

The central fact of capitalist production is the *alienation* of workers from both the process and the product of their labour. With the development of industrialisation, the division of labour which began in earlier eras is carried much further. Work is removed from the home or village to separate large-scale institutions – the factory, the office, the school. Control of work is removed from workers and placed in the hands of management. The conception and execution of work are separated, and workers no longer control the product of their labour (Braverman, 1974). (For a detailed discussion of the concept of alienation, see Schacht, 1971.)

In the process, what workers produce is 'consolidated ... into an objective power above [them]', and they 'become more and more enslaved under a power alien to them' (Marx, cited in Freedman, 1961: 235). Thus alienation (the separation of workers from what they produce) becomes *domination* (the control of workers by owners and managers). As argued above (p. 48), this domination has both a material and an ideological dimension, being constructed in relationships of production and power but being played out in ideologies and discourses and hence being embedded in people's consciousness.

Ideologies and discourses are central to the process of capitalist reproduction. In any historical period, dominant explanations emerge which serve the interests of ruling groups. The post-Fordist problematic is a clear example of this hegemonic process. 'Restructuring' is portrayed as a developmental process. There may be a severe economic crisis, but problems can be overcome by moving to more flexible and competitive forms of production. Luckily, new technologies are available to assist the transition to new forms of work. All workers have to do is to behave rationally and cooperate, and the transition will be smooth. The role of education and training is to develop 'human capital' with the appropriate 'competencies' for flexible production. A new educational discourse appears, built around concepts like 'competency', 'inputs' and 'outputs', and 'assuring quality', which construct educators' understanding of their work (Lingard, 1991: 29–31).

But the reproduction of capitalism is not a smooth process; it is a continually contested one. Capitalism is a system of domination, but one that is continually challenged as ordinary people struggle to maintain or extend control over their lives. As we have seen in previous chapters, the notion of contestation can be linked to the observation that all social life has a learning dimension. That learning can be emancipatory, producing recognition, 'critical consciousness', a movement towards more equitable and just social relationships. Or the learning can be dominative, reproducing oppressive and exploitative relationships and ideologies. In most actual social situations there is probably a mixture of critical and reproductive learning. A vital analytical task for 'radical' adult educators is to sift the recognition from the reproduction. This requires an examination of concrete situations. The next section attempts such an analysis, in relation to economic and workplace 'restructuring' in Australia.

## Adult learning and education in a reorganising capitalism

The role of education and learning in a restructuring capitalism needs to be analysed at both the 'macro' and the 'micro' levels, at the level of policy formation and at the point of practice in particular sites. This, of course, is an enormous task, and only a few indicative points can be made here.

At the macro level, the changing role of the state in Australia and other established capitalist countries has had a determining effect on the direction of educational policy. The globalisation of production has transformed the welfare state into the 'competitive state'. The perceived need of governments to keep their economies inter-nationally competitive has resulted in 'the state itself having to act more and more like a market player' (Cerny, 1990: 230, cited in Yeatman, 1993: 5). Internally, the function of the state changes from the delivery of public services, perceived as the universal rights of citizens, to the fostering of private sector production and the manage-ment of a continually contracting public sector. As Yeatman has noted, this transformation in the role of the state has a number of effects. The first has already been noted: public servants become economic managers rather than service deliverers and client ad-vocates. Secondly, the 'shared collegial culture' and the hierarchical seniority system of the welfare state public service is supplanted by an individualistic, competitive and careerist style of work imported from the private sector. Thirdly, the relatively open competition of interest groups for public resources which characterised the welfare state has been replaced by a more remote and opaque style of decision-making. Decisions are often made at the national level by tripartite groups purportedly representing all workers, all employers and government. Fourthly, public services are more closely 'targeted'. 'Essentially what happens is that [the services] are cut back in relation to claims on them, which means that the quality of service declines, and those who can afford to "choose" opt out of the public system and pay for a private service.' A process of 'recommodification' develops, as public services are privatised and put back into the market (Yeatman, 1993: 5–7).

These changes operate across capitalist countries. However, there are important differences between the role of the state under extreme economic rationalist governments like the Thatcher or Reagan Governments and social democratic regimes such as the Labor Government that held office in Australia from 1983 until 1996. Hard-line economic rationalist governments simply wish to reduce the role of the state as much as possible. Social democratic governments retain some commitment, however compromised, to social justice goals. They attempt to 'create a more efficient and effective public sector by appropriating private sector models of management', and they rely heavily on tripartite activity in policy formation (Knight et al., 1991: 13). In Australia, this 'corporate managerialist' style of state action afforded working people some protection against the worst excesses of a reorganising capitalism. However, by setting up a closed, hierarchical, tripartite style of decision-making,[2] and by appropriating much of the economic rationalist ground, Australian Labor Governments, at both State and Federal level, demobilised the labour movement, as well as encouraging conservative political parties, and capital, to move further to the right. (For discussion of this issue, see Ewer et al., 1991; Knight et al., 1991: 15–16; Pusey, 1991; Horne, 1992; Rees et al., 1993: 15–102).

The competitive state, of conservative or social democratic stripe, seeks to transform education from a citizen's right into an instrument of economic policy. A revived human capital theory conceives people as instruments of production, 'as objects to whom value, for both the individual and society, is added through education and training' (Lingard, 1991: 30). The state develops a more comprehensive and controlling approach to education policy-making. In Australia in the 1980s, a series of Government initiatives attempted to construct a comprehensive system of post-school education closely linked to production. An expanded university system with closer links to business was to focus on economically useful research, and professional education. An expanded and better-funded technical and further education sector was to provide vocational training for the rest of the primary labour force (para-professions, technicians, trades people, white-collar workers). A vocationalised community adult education, an increasing proportion of it provided by private agencies (many of these linked to church-based charities), was to provide labour market training for the secondary labour force and the unemployed, at the same time attempting to fulfil its traditional 'access' function. The most radical conception was of a comprehensive system of workplace reform, which linked workplace education to changes in work organisation, and which required employers to devote a percentage of payroll to employee training. Predictably, the implementation of these educational changes has been complex and contested. I will focus on only one dimension of the changes, the learning dimension of workplace reform.

Under the Labor Government economic policy rested on an 'accord' between unions, business and government around the need for economic restructuring. In the accord process, an attempt was made to develop a more coherent and planned approach to industry and labour market policy. This approach, most clearly articulated in a 1987 document authored by Left unionists (ACTU/TDC, 1987), advocated a planned rationalisation and development of the economy by business, government and trade unions. Economic recovery, it was argued, depended on the rebuilding of manufacturing industry through the adoption of sophisticated technology and the development of new forms of work organisation. Underpinning this approach was the notion of the systematic development of the skills of the workforce through education and training.

The strength of this approach was that it saw industry and workplace restructuring as complex social processes, and thus provided a useful counter to the ideological and technicist prescriptions of the free-marketeers. It accepted that increasing productivity involved more than the application of new technology or the development of new skills, that it also entailed changing work practices, and consequently involved fundamental shifts in workplace power relations and ways of thinking. Further, this approach recognised that what happens at the 'micro' level of the workplace is influenced by decisions taken at the 'macro' level of the corporation, national economy and international economy (ACTU/TDC, 1987; Mathews, 1989a and 1989b).

The actual implementation of workplace restructuring in Australia under the Labor Government, however, emphasised skills formation and neglected the other elements. In major industries like coal, metals, timber, and textiles, employer–union negotiations established restructuring guidelines. Then, in individual workplaces, enterprise agreements were struck which sought to rationalise occupational categories, and establish career paths linked to training. The emphasis in these agreements was on skills formation, and on linking wage increases to improvements in productivity. The approach to skills formation involved audits of workers' existing skills, the setting of competency standards for workers, and the design, delivery and assessment of competency-based training related to the competency standards (Mathews, 1989a).

This approach did not deliver significant changes in productivity. In two important papers Fred Emery (1991a and 1991b) pointed out that the problem with the 'accord' approach to restructuring was that it emphasised skill formation and training, and made no serious attempt to change work organisation. Emery argued that because it did not tackle the crucial issue of 'autocratic work organisation', in which management tries to control the work process and workers resist that control, this restructuring strategy had not increased (and could not increase) productivity sufficiently to make it worthwhile for corporations to invest in productive activities rather than in the money market. Emery claimed that Labor's approach to workplace restructuring ignored the crucial element of worker commitment: why should workers commit themselves to the restructuring process? What's in it for them? (Emery, 1991b: 193–8).

Emery then drew on his encyclopaedic knowledge of twentieth-century studies of workplace change to argue that if those responsible for work are able to organise it, both commitment and productivity increase (Emery, 1991a: 106–8, 1991b: 194–7). He concluded that while there is 'no scientific problem about what to do to rectify low productivity and poor quality of products, there is obviously a social problem in the changing of work organisation. ... The closer we get to making changes at the workface, the more people become concerned with shared visions, trust and values' between workers and managers. It was a problem of 'who is going to bell the cat' (Emery, 1991b: 197). The implication was that the issue of changing worker–management relations had been avoided by management, unions and government because it was too difficult. Studies of workplace reform under the Labor Government support Emery's contention.

In a study of thirty-three workplaces, Curtain and his colleagues (1991) found that the implementation of workplace reform was hindered by the following factors:

• Participants' inexperience in consultation, which was often a function of autocratic or confrontational industrial relations traditions.

- Communication problems in multi-ethnic workforces. The provision of literacy programmes was often seen by companies as being 'too expensive'.
- Participants' excessive expectations of the workplace change process.
- Training bottlenecks.
- Confusion of workplace reform and organisational change.

The studies found that the latter, involving 'cost minimisation', 'downsizing', 'job shedding', 'efficiency gains', was relatively easy to implement; but real changes in power relations and skill development in workplaces were much more difficult to achieve.

Emery's and Curtain's conclusions about the complex and conflictual nature of workplace reform and learning have been confirmed for me in research I have conducting over the past several years on the learning dimension of workplace change in an Australian open-cut coal mine.

A few years ago, as part of an effort to 'restructure' the mine and make it more productive, management decided it wanted to foster more positive worker–management relations. In open-cut mines, draglines dig up the earth, and mechanised shovels load the earth on to large Euclid trucks. One day the workers who drive the Euclids in this mine came on shift to find the local sign-writer painting names on three new trucks. It turned out that the mine management had staged a competition to name the new trucks and a new shovel. The winning entry was 'Snow White and the Seven Dwarfs'. The shovel was to be called Snow White and the trucks named after three of the Seven Dwarfs: Dopey, Sleepy and Grumpy.

The drivers were taken aback. First of all, none of the workers in the mine had entered the competition, so they were puzzled about who could have won. It turned out that the 'girl in the office' had submitted the winning – and only – entry. But the miners were also irritated that the company, which was continually claiming that it was losing money, and which was supposed to be engaged with the workers in a serious attempt at workplace restructuring, should waste money and time on such a trivial, and manipulative, game. The workers relayed their feelings to the mine manager, who said that in one mine that he'd worked at, the trucks were called after Melbourne

Cup winners, to which one of the workers responded, 'I'd rather be called Phar Lap[3] than bloody Dopey'. Another worker told the manager, 'You won't get any harmony by blokes being called Dopey. "Come in Dopey" on the two-way. How's that going to create harmony?' To which the manager replied, 'Get stuffed' and walked out.

Each of the three truck crews in the mine had a go at the manager about the proposed signs. One crew told the manager that they saw no need to have names on the trucks: 'They've got a number, we're only numbers.' Another crew told the manager that they would refuse to drive the trucks if the dwarf illustrations went on them; yet another crew said they would paint over the signs. Faced with this resistance, management dropped the idea.

Behind this story are the histories of a workplace, a class, a community and a nation. Here I can only try to sketch some of what I see as the essential features of those histories, as they illuminate this particular story. The mine concerned, as is common in the industry, has a conflictual industrial relations history. The incident described above took place in the midst of protracted negotiations over an enterprise agreement. Workers did not want any form of enterprise agreement – the system of award-setting through a government-appointed tribunal had worked reasonably well for miners for many years. The workers in this mine, under massive pressure from the central office of their own union which was pursuing the accommodationist political agenda of the national Labor Government, had reluctantly agreed to enterprise bargaining. The negotiations over this agreement dragged on for three years; the workers I interviewed gave detailed accounts of management bad faith, deception and intimidation in these negotiations. The Snow White story encapsulates all this, and also represents the management as blustering idiots, and in a sense, powerless. This powerlessness has to do with management's inability to seduce or trick miners. At a deeper level – and this is very important in understanding the nature of workplace learning – management failed yet again to make workers into what management wants them to be – compliant production mechanisms. The miners saw through the shallowness of management's ploy, wondered at their stupidity in persisting with it, and delighted in resisting and satirising it. In doing this the workers asserted their own strength and dignity. And in that assertion lies the emancipatory importance of this instance of workers' political learning.

It is useful to mention a few other factors that throw light on this example of workers' political learning. First, the workers in this mine come from an established rural community in which they have strong family and friendship ties. These ties both moderate the miners' militancy but also make them unwilling to trade their social life for increased wages. The workers are attached to a particular way of life, and they fight determinedly, but not altogether successfully, to pre- serve it. Secondly, Australian miners, in common with those in other countries, have strong traditions of industrial militancy and solidarity, and these workers, despite many of them being relatively new to the industry, have been inducted into these traditions. In other words, they have learned the tradition. Thirdly, the sardonic humour dis- played in this story and its telling, and especially the delight in seeing a formally powerful person make a fool of himself, is a national characteristic, formed in the nineteenth century, when convicts and then 'free' workers struggled with landowners and other capitalists in the bush and the cities (see Ward, 1958).

Yet the situation is still more complex.

Workers in this mine, when asked about perceptions of the process of workplace change, painted a picture of management incompetence. In one example management was said to have offered a redundancy package to fitters. Soon after it was realised that the wrong sort of workers had been let go and, as one worker put it, 'they had to re- employ fitters and electricians. ... How bloody stupid can you be?' A little further on in this interview this worker spoke in detail about how the mine's work practices, and productivity, could be improved if management listened to workers. When asked how management responded to workers' suggestions, he said there were three sorts of reactions:

> Sometimes they listen to you with a look on their faces like, 'What the bloody hell would you know'. Mainly because they're fairly well educated and they feel that they are the mining engineers. ... [Then again] you can come up with some things and they probably listen to you and say nothing about it and six months down the track they have done that [i.e. what workers suggest]. But see, it's got to be their idea. ... They don't want anyone else to have thought of it. ... Then you get the other blokes you'll ... say to them, 'Why don't you try this?', ... and they say, 'Oh yeah, bloody oath, that's good, we should be doing this'. But [with these people it] just goes straight through. Not really bloody listening.

The worker here is, of course, going beyond questioning the competence of management and is suggesting that managers appropriate workers' knowledge. This is an example of a continual manifestation in the interviews of the workers' awareness that their perceptions and interests and those of management are fundamentally different.

But it would be inaccurate to claim that workers' present a seamless show of solidarity to management. There are many pressures making for 'seriality', or divisions among workers (Metcalfe, 1988: 86–8, 131–2, 166–70). In this mine, union membership, type of work performed, management inducements and workers' age are particularly potent sources of division, as is difference of interest and perception between workers and those who represent them. During a drawn-out process of enterprise bargaining in the mine, workers and their representatives on the workplace committee negotiating the enterprise agreement continually referred to the difficulties of keeping workers informed about, and supportive of, the negotiation process. Union representatives were said continually to withhold information from their members so as not to prejudice negotiations with management. While workers understood the rationale for this, they still found it frustrating. The interviews also revealed deep unease among workers about the whole union and government-endorsed strategy of replacing industry-wide negotiations on wages and conditions with negotiations at the enterprise level. As one worker put it

> This is what frightens me a bit, that everyone's going to have a different bloody agreement. Because we won't be united any more. ... So who's going to support one another?...

Workers' political learning is determined by their place in the capitalist mode of production, specifically by their 'wage labour relation with those who control the means of production' (Metcalfe, 1988: 131). This relationship between capitalists and workers is, as we have seen, essentially one of domination and subordination. Capitalists and their agents (managers, supervisors, some workplace trainers) view workers as instruments of production and use a variety of means to try to coerce and manipulate workers to be optimally productive. Further, workers are in relationship with each other as well as with capitalists. Worker-to-worker relations are as much serial as collective, they are characterised by 'passive dispersal, interchangeability and potential rivalry' as much as by cooperation and solidarity. This means that the working class is best seen as 'a complex moving relation' which generates 'different and often inconsistent responses' to the 'shared challenge' of capitalism. It is therefore wrong to lionise the working class for its solidarity and resistance, or to berate it for its 'false consciousness' or desire for a comfortable life. Instead, we need to recognise the heterogeneity of forms of working-class consciousness and action, and understand that these emerge as responses to the challenges that workers face in actual lived situations (Metcalfe, 1988: 132–6).

These interviews illustrate these fundamental realities of the process of workplace change in capitalist society. What needs to be understood is that in a capitalist political economy the parties in workplace change have different interests, and that consequently there is bound to be conflict among them. Yet there seems to be little or no recognition by policy-makers of the complex and conflictual nature of workplace reform. The same can be said about the overwhelmingly technicist and managerialist literature on the educational dimension of workplace change. Even when it examines informal learning in the workplace (see, for example, Marsick, 1987; Marsick and Watkins, 1991), this literature assumes that education and learning are technical processes, to be facilitated by professionals on behalf of management. The contradictory and contested dynamics of workplace relations are not explored in any depth. The notion of workers' learning being autonomous and resistant barely appears in this literature. When it does, such learning, and organisation around it, are often seen as problems to be overcome by management. Rarely, however, is this ideological sub-text expressed as baldly as it is by Pierce (1987: 31), who discusses a management training workshop which was designed 'to help managers become more effective in order to avoid unionisation of the workforce'. (For an excellent analysis of the ideological nature of recent US workplace learning literature, see Hart, 1992: 145–54.)

The ideologies of the educational restructuring literature generally operate more subtly. So, for example, in Australia over the past few years a great deal of effort has been put into redesigning vocational education and workplace training curricula so that they more accurately reflect competencies required in workplaces. This effort has largely focused on the technical aspects of identifying competency standards (CS) and designing and delivering competency-based training programmes (CBT). Critiques of the CS/CBT approach, based on analysis of its actual processes and outcomes, tend to be responded to dismissively by CS/CBT advocates. So Hager and Gonczi, who have been involved in the development of competency standards in Australia, respond to John Field's (1991) critique of the implementation of CS/CBT in Britain by arguing that competency analyses are 'not necessarily' atomised and mechanical, that competency-based assessment does not have to reinforce existing workplace hierarchies, and that the development of competency-based standards is not necessarily dominated by business interests (Hager and Gonczi, 1991: 26). Certainly none of these things *has* to happen. But they are likely to, in a capitalist society. And they are more likely to if educators involved in developing the CS/CBT approach to their work in narrowly technical ways have no strategies for linking educational innovations to the complex, contradictory and contested nature of workplace change in a reorganising capitalism.

Radical adult educators need to turn away from the dominant technicist formulation of 'restructuring', and pay attention to what workers, and the unemployed, are actually experiencing and learning in the process of capitalist reorganisation. The interviews discussed above demonstrate that there is a learning dimension to all workplace change, and to workplace life in general. Adult educators often overlook the learning dimension that is integral to social life, so intent are they on constructing 'education'. It is important to recognise that workers construct their own understanding of the dynamics of the places in which they work. Adult educators need to develop an understanding of the dynamics of workers' informal learning – of how and why workers construct particular understandings of their workplaces.

## Beyond capitalist reorganisation

I have argued in this chapter that in Australia and in other western countries during the past decade a complex process of capitalist reorganisation has been transformed, in the minds of policy-makers and many adult educators, into a simplified and mythical notion of 'restructuring'. We are undoubtedly living through the most significant economic reorganisation since the advent of mass production and consumption, and 'scientific' management. But it is highly unlikely that the outcome of this process will simply be the productive, flexible, internationally competitive workplaces touted by their advocates. The social costs of the globally dominant technicist and rationalist approach to restructuring are already massive: high levels of unemployment around the globe and acceptance of mass starvation in Africa, to name just two recent examples.

Adult educators themselves are all too aware of the pernicious effects of the current period of economic restructuring. (For analyses of these effects in Australia, see Ewer et al., 1991; and Horne, 1992.) Many of us have, however uneasily, attempted to respond pragmatically to economically and politically driven changes in education. So we have, for example, worked harder with continually shrinking resources, become more accountable (accepting 'strategic planning' and 'quality assurance'), more oriented to the workplace (embracing skills training and competency-based learning), and more entrepreneurial (indeed, some of us, as consultants, have moved wholly into the market). While these responses are understandable, it is time to look at their costs, and to ask ourselves whether there are not other ways that adult educators can respond to this fundamental economic reorganisation.

One thing that adult educators can do is to understand, and name, the current 'restructuring' for what it is: a significant reorganisation of capitalism. To recognise this is to immediately see that there is no easy way out of the difficult times in which we live. Restructuring is a contested process, in which both capital and labour are trying to protect and extend their interests. Adult educators have a clear choice in this struggle. They can pretend the struggle does not exist, and that 'restructuring' is a technical and rational process. If we take this path, the chances are that our work will, at best, be ineffective. As Fred Emery's analysis and the growing body of data on the outcomes of the 'accord' approach to workplace reform in Australia demonstrate, change strategies which do not take account of the complexities of workplaces will fail. Worse, technicist strategies, by ignoring power relations, often contribute to maintaining or extending (the latter being the more likely in the current environment) oppression and exploitation.

To recognise, and name, capitalist reorganisation for what it is is to begin to resist it and to articulate alternatives. In late twentieth-century capitalism, the development of counter-strategies is an extremely difficult, but still attainable, goal. But the development of effective counter-strategies must begin with a recognition that the real impediment to a just society is the capitalist social order. Capitalism, built as it is on the exploitation of the many by the few, is opposed to the general interest. There will be no secure and long-term reformation of capitalism in the interests of the many. The last two decades should have sharply reminded us of what the whole history of capitalism demonstrates: capitalism is inherently unstable and destructive, and it recovers from its periodic crises by intensifying the exploitation of labour. Under capitalism, gains won by working people are always liable to reversal. Nothing could illustrate this axiom more clearly than the massive shift of wealth from labour to capital, and the recommodification of social services, which occurred in the 1980s.

Recent experience should also teach us that any economic restructuring (even one which, as with the Australian experience, has involved significant input from the labour movement) which is directed by the capitalist state will be, ultimately and primarily, in the interests of capital and against the general interest. This means that there will be, in our time, no 'post-Fordist' or 'post-industrial' nirvana, and that we will continue to live, and struggle, within a political and economic system which is grossly, and ultimately unsustainably, exploitative of people and nature. It also means that each of us faces the choice put to workers in the old union song: 'Whose side are you on?' Do we adult educators choose to work with, and for, capital by accommodating ourselves to, with whatever qualifications and continued rhetorical resistance, the language and techniques of a workplace restructuring which is so clearly driven by the interests of capital? Or do we take the far more difficult path of striving to develop forms of education which really do serve the interests of working people? To pose the choice so baldly in this post-communist, economic rationalist, pragmatic era may seem both unbearably naive and insufferably moralising. But the choice is unavoidable. There is just too much evidence now, from the outcomes of the German middle class's deliberate blindness to Nazism, to Foucault's analyses of the oppressive effects of everyday professional practice, that those who misinterpret the dynamics of capitalism collude in its reproduction.

Yet the choices and decisions of individual adult educators are only a small part of what must be done. The processes of combating capitalism and working towards more just and humane forms of social organisation are complex and contradictory, as the next two chapters demonstrate.

## Notes

1. 'State' is taken here to mean 'the central institutionalisation of social power' which regulates relations between people 'by policy and policing' (Franzway et al., 1989: 52). More specifically, the term is used in the Marxist sense of 'the political means by which the political needs of the economically powerful classes [are] met' (Curthoys, 1988: 36). The position adopted here seeks to avoid the functionalist and determinist difficulties of older Marxist theories of the state by focusing on the ideological and legitimising role of the state, and in particular the way the state constitutes (i.e. establishes or enacts) the very categories (such as education) through which social life is defined (Franzway et al., 1989: 52).

2. Former Labor Prime Minister Keating encapsulated this style in responding to a call by a leading trade unionist for the Australian Senate to amend the 1993–94 Budget. Keating, while acknowledging the right of the unionist to express his organisation's view, suggested that 'the best way to deal with the Government in the Accord [tripartite government/union/business policy-making process] is to deal with it persuasively. And that is, talk to us in private and not in public' (*The Australian*, 28/8/93).

3. A famous Australian racehorse, who died in the United States. Phar Lap is an Australian national symbol of pluck.

CHAPTER 6

. . . . . . . . . . . . . . . . . . . . . . . . . . . . .

# Learning in Brazilian Women's Organisations

To argue, as I did in the last chapter, that learning and education are ultimately determined by broader economic and political forces, is not to sink into a crude determinism. But it is necessary to show the complex ways that this determination works itself through in particular situations. The account of workers' learning in the previous chapter provides one example of this. The analysis of Brazilian women's learning in this chapter provides another example.

In her study of Brazilian women's organisations in the period 1964–89, Sonia Alvarez (1990b) argues that we need to examine the macro-economic, the micro-political and the discursive dimensions of social movement activity (see especially, 1990b: 38–55, 57–9, 260–9). Alvarez's particular interest is in the gender dimension of these movements and struggles in non-revolutionary situations (1990b: 3–4, 13, 264). My broad interest in this book is in the learning dimension of emancipatory social struggles. In what follows an attempt will be made to read this learning dimension into Alvarez's account of Brazilian women's movements. Particular attention will be given to situating discussion of the learning of emancipatory discourses within an analysis of broader political and economic developments and local micro-political factors.[1]

## The broad political and economic context: authoritarianism, resistance, *abertura* and *peripheria*

On 1 April 1964 a military junta deposed the populist government of Jao Goulart. Conservative upper- and middle-class women's organisations played an important role in preparing the ideological ground for the coup with a series of orchestrated demonstrations. 'Armed with crucifixes and rosaries, thousands of upper- and middle-class women paraded through the streets of Brazil's major cities, imploring the military to perform its "manly duty" and restore order and stability to the nation.' The last of these marches occurred the day before the coup (1990b: 5–6).

In power, the junta sent the women 'back to the kitchens' but continued to use 'traditional symbols of feminine piety and spiritual superiority, morality and motherhood' to justify its repressive political and economic project. The junta's political strategy generated resistance from organised sections of civil society. In 1967 and 1968 workers, students and women held massive demonstrations against the regime. These protests generated further repression, including political assassinations and torture. But this terror failed to crush the resistance (1990b: 37). Over the next several years people's organisations expanded their activities, forcing the military regime to initiate a process of political liberalisation from above (*abertura* in Portuguese), leading to a long period of transition culminating in the restoration of formal democracy in 1985 (1990b: 11).

The seeds of popular resistance lay in the junta's economic strategy, which

> rested on an accelerated industrialisation drive fuelled by multinational and transnationalised domestic capital investment and debt-financed state investment, supported by regressive wage policies and tight controls on labour. ... [A] policy of deliberate income concentration [in favour of the upper and middle classes], aimed at expanding the domestic market for durable consumer goods, coupled with the systematic political exclusion and repression of those most adversely affected by these policies ... (Alvarez, 1990b: 37, 51)

This strategy generated rapid economic growth throughout the 1970s, achieved through the gross exploitation of labour. The usurpation of peasant lands to facilitate the development of capital intensive agriculture, together with the expansion of manufacturing industry, led to massive rural–urban migration. Most labour migrants settled on the outskirts of cities (*peripheria* in Portuguese), often on land 'sold' illegally by speculators and lacking roads, water, electricity, sewage, health and educational facilities. With families unable to survive solely on male wages, women were also forced into the workforce and/or into some form of domestic production for subsistence and/or the market (1990b: 44–7). Responsibility for trying to do something about the lack of urban services in the *peripheria* also fell primarily on women, both because women were traditionally cast in the role of family sustainer and caregiver, and because men's waged work and travel to and from their jobs took them away from their homes for most of their waking hours.

The conditions of life in the *peripheria* generated extensive local political action by women. From the mid-1960s onwards, women's organisations were formed in the urban settlements, involving hundreds of thousands of Brazilian working-class women in self-help and protest activities. During the same period many middle-class women also became involved in community organisations and other feminist initiatives. It is to an examination of the micro-politics, discursive practices and learning dimension of these women's movements that I now turn. (For further analysis of this period of Brazil's history, see Alves, 1985; Packenham, 1986. For contrasting analyses of the transition from military rule to parliamentary democracy in Latin America in general during this period, see Herman and Petras, 1985; and Cammack, 1986.)

## Micro-politics, discursive practices and adult learning

Alvarez's study seeks to explain the emergence and development of progressive women's organisations and movements in the period of repression, economic crisis and transition to democracy in Brazil in the period 1964–89. Her particular interest is in the relationship between political change and changes in women's consciousness. Drawing on social movement theory, Alvarez notes that there is no automatic relationship between changes in material conditions and the development of mass political consciousness and action. She argues that in the 1960s and 1970s in Brazil a crucial consciousness-raising role was performed by oppositional discourses of human rights, social justice, equality and liberation, which had their source in the Brazilian Left, Latin American liberation theology and international feminism. The new discourses played 'a crucial role in shaping the subjective possibilities' for political action 'by [challenging] oppressive conditions for subordinate social groups and classes, fashioning new social and political identities, and providing ... ethical rationales for engaging in anti-status quo behaviour and political action' (Alvarez, 1990b: 58). But these ideological forces interacted in complex ways with micro-political factors.

Three such factors were particularly important: male domination in both church-based and secular Left organisations, which heightened women's awareness of gendered inequality; the organisational resources provided by the new groups; and political liberalisation after 1974 which created a climate which legitimated debate and action on women's issues, and which forced all political parties to lend at least rhetorical support to women's issues (1990b: 3, 57–8). (For further discussion of Brazilian social movements – including workers' and ecological movements – during this period, see Alves, 1984; Mainwaring and Viola, 1984; Kowarick, 1985; Vink, 1985; Viola, 1988; Mainwaring, 1989; Mulligan, 1994. Slater (1985), locates Brazilian and other Latin American social movements within a wider intellectual and political debate about 'new' social movements. Aspects of this debate are discussed in the Conclusion to this book.)

## The church, the Left and women's organisations

Until the 1960s the Brazilian church had been a pillar of reaction. It had fiercely opposed Goulart's mild liberal reforms and had actively supported the 'family, God and liberty' campaign that helped bring the military junta to power. But the liberation theology that emerged from the Second Vatican Council (1962–65) and the Medellin conference of Latin American Bishops in 1968 triggered a struggle between conservative and radical ideologies in the Brazilian church (Alvarez, 1990b: 60–1).

Vatican II redefined the church's mission in the world, enabling the secular to be placed alongside the religious, and the political alongside the spiritual. The church was urged to exercise moral leadership in civil society, to act as a catalyst and prophet to promote justice. The Medellin conference articulated the idea of the Church of the Poor, a church that would stand with the poor and oppressed. During the 1970s, in the face of massive human rights abuses throughout South and Central America (see Galeano, 1989, 1992), including against many church members, the church sharpened its critique of institutionalised violence and authoritarianism. By the mid-1970s the Brazilian Bishops'

Conference 'had become a major oppositional force, shielding the politically persecuted and fostering community organisations and mobilisation among the poor' (Alvarez, 1990b: 61–2).

A particularly important part of the progressive shift in the Brazilian church was the creation of Christian Base Communities (*Commuidades Eclesias de Base* or CEBs). These groups of fifteen to forty parishioners met together regularly to discuss the new social teachings of the church. By the late 1980s there were over 100,000 of these groups in Brazil. The social gospel of the progressive church also brought many nuns and priests into direct contact with the concrete conditions of working people's lives. These experiences radicalised clergy and led to the articulation of a liberation theology which combined Christian teaching and critical sociological analysis which drew on such sources as dependency theory and Marxism. The radical pastoral work of the Brazilian church was also informed by the theories of Paulo Freire, who during his work with slum dwellers and peasants in and around Recife in the 1960s, developed an educational methodology which helped the oppressed to identify and work out ways of dealing with the sources of their oppression (Alvarez, 1990b: 62, 70).

The reformed church also advocated an increased public role for women. Yet there was a deep-seated essentialist view of women in the Brazilian church, even in its more radical sections. Women were seen as wives, mothers and nurturers. Theoretical and rhetorical affirmations of women's equality with men were not matched by changes in behaviour. Women performed most of the 'infrastructural work' for church and other community groups: catering, cleaning, sweeping. Alvarez concluded from her own extensive observations of Sao Paulo mothers' clubs that they functioned primarily as 'ladies auxiliaries' to parish organisations: 'I did not see or hear of a single club that was created with the intention of helping women gain consciousness, or act politically, as women' (Alvarez, 1990b: 68–9).

There were similar problems with women's position in the Brazilian Left. The defeat of armed struggle in the 1960s and 1970s caused many on the Left to discard the 'vanguardist' notion that had informed the guerrilla groups and to join in the painstaking and long-term political work (frequently referred to as 'ants' labour' [*trabalho de formiginha*] by Alvarez's informants) of community-based organisations. Many Left women began working as *assessoras* (consultants) in church-linked mothers' clubs and youth groups, taking with them into these organisations the critique of patriarchal behaviour they had developed in Left organisations, where they had experienced a similar marginalisation to that of women in church-based organisations (Alvarez, 1990b: 70–5).

An understanding of the contradictory progressive and patriarchal ideologies underpinning Brazilian community-based women's organisations is important, because the ambiguities and contradictions in these ideologies helped to shape their members' political learning. As we will see below, women in these organisations increasingly came to critique patriarchal ideas and practices and to assert their own distinctive gender interests and perspectives.

## Social action and learning in women's organisations

From the early 1960s Brazilian women began to organise around a range of issues: low wages for domestic servants, the lack of services in the *peripheria*, the rapidly rising cost of living, human rights abuses. From the mid-1970s local women's organisations began to work together in city-wide, regional and national campaigns. During 1973 mothers' clubs in a Sao Paulo parish conducted a survey of consumer prices among local women. The results of the survey were published as an open letter to government authorities. The letter denounced the miserable conditions of life in the *peripheria*, and demanded price freezes on staples, salary increases corresponding to rises in the cost of living, an immediate salary bonus of 25 per cent, and the establishment of municipal food distribution centres, facilities for consumer cooperatives and day-care centres for the children of working women. The survey/open letter tactic proved attractive to other women's groups. Further, expanded surveys were conducted in 1975 and 1976 (Alvarez, 1990b: 84–5).

Day-care for children was an important focus of women's political activity in the 1970s. Both working-class and middle-class women, entering the waged labour force in large numbers, demanded publicly provided day-care, often using the same survey/public letter tactic employed in the cost of living movement. But the demand for day-care, and the very establishment of women's organisations, could emerge in indirect ways. In the Sao Paulo neighbourhood of Jardim Miriam a mothers' club was established in the late 1960s at the initiative of Johnson and Johnson, whose sales representatives came to the neighbourhood to promote sanitary napkins, teach women to use them, etc. The sales representatives also promoted lectures on women's reproductive cycle, menstruation and so on. After the Johnson and Johnson people left, we began holding sewing lessons for local women at the church which we combined with lectures on different subjects of interest to women. (Interview with two founding members of the organisation, cited in Alvarez, 1990b: 85)

Alvarez found that 'participation in the club itself led women to formulate new, gender-related political demands. At meetings, women typically discussed problems encountered in their daily lives, in their marriages, in feeding and caring for their families' (1990b: 86). As in the Australian situations discussed in Chapter 4 of this book, activities centred around children soon led to other activities as 'neighbourhood women began to value the ability to come together to discuss their shared problems and devise collective solutions' (ibid.). Again the founding members take up the story:

The mothers' club had existed for a long time before the creche movement began. The women always brought their children to the club meetings and at first we rotated taking care of them among ourselves. Around 1970 or so, we began to think of a place where we could leave our children to be taken care of when we had other things to do. ... Discussions continued and the idea emerged to organise a group of women who would go talk to the prefecture. ... We didn't even know what we would say there, but we went anyway, six of us, and we told them of the need for day care in our neighbourhood. Two social workers appeared and suggested we circulate a petition in the neighbourhood. So we did. (Cited in Alvarez, 1990b: 86).

When the women returned with their completed petition, the workers referred them to the 'official' neighbourhood organisation (the SAB), established under the Goulart regime in the 1950s. The demand for day-care sat with this organisation for 'five whole years'. And meanwhile, the women reported, 'we were all waiting for the prefecture to come and build a day-care centre because we had asked for one'. Eventually the women realised that they 'had been lied to' by the workers. This realisation had come about because 'other things were happening in the neighbourhood by then that helped us to gain political consciousness'.

In the mid-1970s the new social emphasis in the local Catholic church had led to the establishment of a new community-based organisation in Jardim Miriam. Many of the members of the mothers' club also joined the new organisation and in it they became involved in a range of campaigns – for elementary schools, health-care facilities and day-care. In these campaigns the women encountered militant opposition groups and Christian charity groups. From these activists the women learned how to deal with government agencies: 'If we're there pressuring them, things will happen. If we leave it up to them we'll never get anything we need in the neighbourhood.' Once they recognised this the women decided to by-pass the SAB and began to organise weekly trips to the municipal bureau of social welfare (SEBES).

In the late 1970s the Struggle for Day Care Group recruited more members from a local sewing class which had been established by a radical priest. The Struggle group also developed strong contacts with the more radical social workers at SEBES who kept the members informed of the progress of their demand for a day-care centre. 'We would go there, fifteen or twenty or more of us, whenever we thought things were being held up … as mothers we demanded the right to a place to leave our children.' Women who were organising for day-care in another neighbourhood began to come to the Jardim Miriam group, to learn from their experiences.

According to Alvarez, there were a number of distinctive features of the Jardim Miriam experience, which it shared with other women's groups in the *peripheria*. The first is that while there was important learning for the women in the day-care campaign, it was of a 'personally transformative' kind. 'For many women', Alvarez argues, 'participation in community organisations is a pleasant experience, an empowering experience, one that breaks the monotony of their daily housework routines and enables them to "learn about the world" from other women' (1990b: 87). This contact enabled women to identify 'shared concerns, common needs'. But those needs 'were not defined in terms of the larger political-economic system nor on the basis of an articulate theoretical, or ideological understanding of that system'. Rather, these women 'developed political claims *on the basis of their day-to-day lived experience as women. …* They began to organise for urban improvements that would facilitate their jobs as wives and mothers' (1990b: 88, emphasis added).

A second feature of the Jardim Miriam campaigns was the

important role played by outside activists in facilitating local political organising. 'Popular movement participants from adjoining neighbourhoods, charity workers, political activists and state social workers all furnished key organisational resources and information to local women's self-help efforts in the urban periphery' (Alvarez, 1990b: 88). But many government-sponsored organisations which could have supported community groups like the Jardim Miriam Struggle group did not. This apathy or refusal had the paradoxical effect of helping women to become more self-reliant and activist. They learned that if they did not do the organising it would not get done.

## A distinctive gender interest

At the same time that women in the Sao Paulo *peripheria* were becoming politically active, feminism was re-emerging among middle-class women in the city. In the late 1960s women in student and other Left organisations began to meet in small groups, usually to discuss Marxist-feminist texts. For some years discussion in these groups centred on the relationship of feminism and socialism and the dominant view was that women had no interests apart from the general popular interest in overthrowing the military regime. But by the mid-1970s both middle-class and working-class women were beginning to share their experiences 'as wives, mothers, lovers, *as women*' (Alvarez, 1990b: 100). Working-class women in community organisations

> often discussed problems they shared about their marriages, their sexual lives, their desire to control fertility, their thirst for more information about the world outside the domestic sphere to which they were usually confined, their relationship to family and community—subjects that middle-class feminists themselves initially thought would be taboo among women of the popular classes. (1990b: 100–1)

Socialist feminists also began to distinguish between class and gender oppression. A feminist activist recalled that her group's work in distributing the feminist newspaper *Nos Mulheres* (Us Women)

> was also a moment for consciousness-raising with the women's groups with which we had contact, the result was that, little by little, we confirmed, in practice, the universality of certain sensations: the uneasiness or unrest of 'being female'; the feeling of suffering some injustice without necessarily exactly understanding its proportions'. (Alvarez, 1990b: 101–2)

By 1977 an editorial in that same newspaper was asserting that the feminist struggle 'went beyond' the class struggle and that 'woman also suffers a specific oppression because of the simple fact of being a woman' – and then went on to spell out in some detail what that oppression entailed (1990b: 102).

During these years working-class and middle-class women were also coming together in neighbourhood organisations and in the increasing number of umbrella organisations that grew up around the day-care and cost of living campaigns. In these years, too, the first city-wide and national women's congresses were held, and International Women's Day began to be celebrated (Alvarez, 1990b: 89–108). A clear distinction emerged between two tendencies in the women's movement, the feminist and the feminine. This distinction was spelt out in a newspaper account of the second Sao Paulo women's congress in 1980:

> If feminist, the major preoccupation is the discussion of women's specific problems, regardless of her class or area of political action. In this case, general struggles are important and should be stimulated as areas of action for women, but only if their militancy does not make them forget their condition as women, who are consequently doubly oppressed: as women and as a class. If feminine, its central preoccupation is to discuss the general struggles (for water, sewage, electricity, day care, etc.) and the participation of women in these struggles. The specificity of women's struggles is not important before the struggle of all of society. (Cited in Alvarez, 1990b: 124–5)

At the second congress the differences between these two positions were so sharp that at one point their adherents came to blows (Alvarez, 1990b: 123). Nevertheless, the congress was able to articulate some goals acceptable to both sides: contraception information to be available in health clinics; universal state provision of non-coercive, accessible family planning; the creation of a forum to debate the abortion issue; the continuation of the struggle for day-care and occupational training for women (1990b: 124).

As the 1980s progressed there was an increasing shift in women's organisations from seeing women's struggles simply as part of a broad movement against dictatorship and for democracy, to seeing that there were specific women's issues that had to be dealt with: issues around sexuality, reproductive rights, violence against women, divorce, child-care, the domestic division of labour (Alvarez, 1990b: 111–12).

Out of these differences and struggles among women came important learning. The congresses and other coordinated initiatives provided spaces in which women from different backgrounds could learn from each other and come to understand that they needed each other. The alternative newspaper *Em Tempo*, commenting on the first Sao Paulo women's congress, referred to that forum's 'capacity to create a climate of enthusiasm, solidarity and trust, and to also touch the emotions of participants' and how this had 'led to spontaneous demands that "we cannot say goodbye now ... we cannot wait until the next Congress; we must continue to struggle together"' (Alvarez, 1990b: 115). Cross-class organisational work and forums also provided opportunities for women to learn by articulating their developing consciousness of previously repressed areas of their lives. So, for example, a working-class woman's account of the exploitation of her sexuality, spoken at the second congress:

> Women suffer much more with problems of sex. I married when I was fourteen years old. My father said that I was three years older on the documents. I have been living with my husband for thirty years. Sometimes I rebel and wonder why I ever got married. When the girls were born, I slept with them, after working like a dog all day long. He never helped me, slept in the other room. Then, when the girls were still, he would come and get me. He would fulfil himself and that was it. Me, never. I know I always repressed that side, sex. But because of my daughters I put up with everything. I live for them. (1990b: 114).

(For further analysis of Brazilian women's movements and feminism during this period see Alvarez, 1989, 1990a; and Sarti, 1989. For discussion of Latin American feminism more generally, see Flora, 1984, and for analysis of the broader historical and theoretical context of Brazilian feminism, see Saffioti, 1978.)

## Complexities of emancipatory learning

One of the great strengths of Alvarez's book is that it shows how these gains in consciousness on the part of women were not straightforwardly developmental, that learning and consciousness-raising were difficult, ambiguous and contested. The story of the women's group in Jardim Miriam illustrates this complexity. In the late 1970s the domestic sewing class in the church-based women's organisation at Jardim Miriam was transformed into an occupational training course.

External funds were obtained, industrial sewing machines installed and 20–25 women enrolled (Alvarez, 1990b: 126–7). The three middle-class organisers of this course wanted it to have a political dimension:

> We were going to 'develop' these women, teach them skills so that they could become incorporated in productive labour. We decided to hold discussions about why women needed to gain skills and financial independence, why working outside the home was important for women. (1990b: 127)

Simple texts were developed, which were then read and discussed in 'theoretical' sessions. The organisers were trying to locate skills training within a wider political and economic context – they wanted the learners to relate their sewing work to their family, domestic labour and their place in the workforce. But, one of the organisers recalled:

> within the first three months everything we thought the course would be fell apart. ... The course became their space. They spoke much more freely about a number of things from the start than we did ... things like sexuality, their intimate relationships ... things we hadn't anticipated discussing in the group. (1990b: 127)

At the learners' request, class discussions focused less on work and more on such issues as children's education, women's socialisation and family relationships. In early 1980 a woman doctor joined the class and at the women's request began leading discussions on women's bodies and health; these topics became the focus of the class in its second year. This new focus attracted more than four times the number of participants than the 'contextualised' sewing class had (Alvarez, 1990b: 128). But the direction of the discussion group disturbed some of the more conservative church women in the group who 'were scandalised by the stories of back-alley abortions, extra-marital relations, and sexual relations in general that typified the course's theoretical discussions by 1980–1981'. These women complained to the local priest who told the organisers that they had not 'respected the limits of the parishioners' and must stop discussing such controversial issues. The organisers then engaged in debate with the priest, telling him that

> he thought our work was absolutely secondary within the political work of the church, [we reminded him] that the women in our group did all the support work for the church but received no support for their own

issues in return. ... The women were the foundation of the church's activities in the neighbourhood ... they cleaned, cooked ... even did [the priest's] laundry. (1990b: 128)

While the priest, a strong advocate of liberation theology, appeared happy for his female parishioners to be extended on issues related to social class and the need for 'general social transformation', he was most uncomfortable with the educational work that dealt with gender-specific issues and which challenged patriarchal church practices and doctrine. After several heated discussions with the priest, and extensive deliberations among the group's organisers, the women's group left the church and formed an autonomous women's organisation. But many neighbourhood women disagreed with this move and partici-pation in the society declined. In early 1983 the organisers phased out the course and established a woman's centre which focused on domestic violence and rape. By late 1983 the parish priest and some local male community organisers were attacking the centre for its 'bourgeois feminism', accusing it of promoting lesbianism, destroying family life and misusing funds. These attacks led some women to leave the group and to return to the church. By mid-1985 the women's centre had ceased functioning and women were again attending sewing classes in the church (Alvarez, 1990b: 128–32).

## Women's movements and political liberalisation

In the 1980s, complexity piled upon complexity in the Brazilian women's movement. Alvarez analyses these complexities in detail; they can only be discussed briefly here. From the 1974 congressional elections, when the tame opposition party unexpectedly became the bearer of the people's protest at military dictatorship and did well at the polls, Brazil was engaged in a process of *abertura* or political liberalisation. In 1979 the military junta split the political opposition into five parties and scheduled new congressional elections for 1982 (Alvarez, 1990b: 145–6, 151–3).

The creation of political parties drew many women's energies away from community organising and into electoral politics. This both directed energy away from cultural and consciousness-raising work (see, for example, Alvarez, 1990b: 150, 160) and exacerbated political differences in and among women's organisations (1990b: 138). At the same time feminists were able to use electoral politics as a space for organisation and education around women's issues, endorsing candidates who supported feminist platforms (1990b: 143).

The complex and ambiguous impact of electoral politics on women's groups can be illustrated through an examination of the experience of women in Jardim Miriam during the 1981–82 election campaign. The dominant parties in Jardim Miriam during this campaign were the *Partido dos Trabalhadores* (Workers Party, known as PT) and the government party, the PDS. The PT was the only party with a visible presence in Jardim Miriam and other *peripheria* settlements, where it organised party nuclei which were staffed by the same activists who had been instrumental in establishing neighbourhood organisations, especially those linked to the progressive Catholic church. The neighbourhood activists were attracted by the PT's stated commitment to building a working-class party 'from the base up', a party which would become the parliamentary voice of community movements.

In 1981–82 the organisers of the Jardim Miriam women's group made 'politics and elections' the focus of the sewing course's theoretical sessions. This appears to have been at the request of group members who expressed an interest in learning about 'this party business'. Church-provided slide shows and films on the electoral process were shown, and discussions held on the platforms of the various political parties, the organisers always coming down in favour of the PT as the only true expression of community and working-class interests. When none of the PT's local lists of candidates included women, members of the sewing class endorsed their own lists of women candidates, all of whom were feminist activists who had addressed the class over the preceding months.

Post-electoral discussion among the Jardim Miriam group's organisers, observation of the group's discussions and studies of other women's groups in the Sao Paulo *peripheria* revealed tensions between electoral activities and other purposes of these groups. Women's group members were generally more interested in discussions of sexuality, women's health, educational provision and other immediate women's and neighbourhood issues than in the election. Many women expressed ignorance of, and distrust in, electoral politics: 'I don't understand anything about parties', 'Politicians only come around here when there are elections and they confuse me even then', 'I don't fool with politics, my husband does'. Electoral politics was often seen by women as self-serving, self-interested and unethical, unlike women's work in neighbourhood groups, which was seen as work in the interests of their families and communities and as not being political. In Jardim Miriam women did not participate actively in the creation of party nuclei, and it appeared that the local PT was not an hospitable place for women. While the Jardim Miriam women's group had designated representatives to the PT, these rarely attended PT meetings and when they did they felt that their contributions were not taken seriously. The stigma that attached to organisations like the Jardim Miriam women's group in the early 1980s seems to have carried over into the PT, where women's work was often perceived as 'apolitical' or 'divisive', 'frivolous' or even 'dangerous' (Alvarez, 1990b: 154–8, 161–77).

In November 1982 the major Centre-Right opposition party won a majority in the congressional elections (Alvarez, 1990b: 162, 198). In 1983, under pressure from the International Monetary Fund (IMF) to adopt 'structural adjustment' measures to deal with Brazil's economic crisis and the gargantuan debt generated by the 'economic miracle' of the 1960s and 1970s, the Brazilian government moved peremptorily from a position of hostility to family planning to articulating a coherent family planning programme that reflected what many feminists had been demanding. This move at first confounded Brazilian feminists, accustomed as they were to distrusting the state. In the succeeding months feminists had to unlearn the assumption that any state-sponsored family planning initiative would be coercive, and develop ways of engaging with and influencing state policy. Alvarez gives a detailed account of this process and concludes that the women's movement had some success in making this adjustment (1990b: 178–97).

But as the feminist movement learned to work 'in and against the state' on the family planning and other issues, moving from a politics of resistance and protest to a politics of influencing policy, new complications emerged. The continuing economic crisis, the intractable foreign debt problem and the IMF's draconian 'remedy' circumscribed the state's capacity to meet women's demands. The 'masculinity' of Brazilian politics meant that women's programmes, such as childcare, were often the first to be cut, such cuts being justified by reference to women's traditional roles (childcare, for example, was said to be 'women's work'). By the late 1980s there was a strong feeling among feminists interviewed by Alvarez that 'institutions had swallowed up the movement' and that many women formerly active in the women's movement had been 'conservatised' and 'neutralised' through their participation in political parties and state institutions. Intergenerational divisions were emerging between 'historic' and younger feminists. Divisions, too, developed between 'cultural' feminists who maintained that they could best influence the world through the arts and the media, and activists who continued to do more traditional educational and political work. Splits were also developing between black and white feminists, with the former creating their own organisations (Alvarez, 1990b: 221–34).

By the late 1980s there had been a general failure to develop 'organic' ties between political parties and women's organisations, although there were more successful attempts to build links between the latter and trade unions. There were some successful examples of coalition-building among women's groups and these had a positive impact on government policies on day-care and family planning. But attempts to build a national women's organisation were undermined by political differences and manipulation. There were innovative state-sponsored attempts to deal with violence against women, including the establishment of police precincts staffed solely by women. But such initiatives seemed to undermine and de-activate existing autonomous groups concerned with violence against women. Finally, many of the most experienced and effective movement activists were drawn into the state apparatus (Alvarez, 1990b: 234–47). (For further discussion of the complexities of *arbetura* politics in Brazil see Schmink, 1981; Latin America Bureau, 1982; Caldeira, 1986–87; Keck, 1986–87; Schneider, 1986; Danaher and Shellenberger, 1995.)

## Conclusions and directions

What then does the Brazilian experience tell us about the relationship of adult learning and social movement activity?

While economic and political changes may create the material conditions for social movement activity, these changes do not necessarily generate such activity. For people to become actively involved in social movements something must happen to their consciousness – they must see that action is necessary and possible. Alvarez points to the crucial role of the oppositional discourses of human rights,

social justice, feminism and liberation theology in creating the subjective conditions for political action in Brazilian women's movements.
She also gives a detailed account of the micro-politics of these movements. It is these emphases that makes Alvarez's book so interesting
for adult educators. Her analytical framework takes account of both
macro-economic and micro-political factors. Her focus on discourse
provides a bridge between this rich contextualised analysis of social
movement activity and an analysis of adult learning, because the
process of engaging with oppositional discourses is a *learning* process.
But Alvarez provides little detailed information about these learning
processes in individuals, which is the sort of data that we must have
if we are to build up a rich picture of learning in social movements.

In this chapter I have tried to 'read in' a learning dimension to
Alvarez's data, but have been constrained by the lack of detailed
information on learning processes in the women's movements. In
this section I will attempt to theorise this learning dimension more
coherently. The starting point in this theorisation is contestation
theory, which points to the universality of domination and of resistance to domination. In Chapter 4 we noted the *continually contested,
complex, ambiguous, and contradictory* nature of this struggle and also
noted its learning dimension. As we have seen in this chapter, Brazil's
recent history is a textbook case of this dialectic of oppression and
resistance. In 1964 the mild reformism of the Goulart years was
terminated by a military coup. The junta used conservative women's
organisations and traditional feminine symbolism in its ideological
offensive before the coup. By 1967 the authoritarianism of the state
had generated resistance by workers, women and students. This
resistance was stiffened by the junta's economic strategy which
pushed peasants off the land, created labour reserves on the outskirts
of the cities and forced men and women to work for below-subsistence wages. This in turn made women's labour essential for the
survival of working-class families, and generated political activity
around a range of issues: the cost of living, the need for urban
services, childcare, the low wages of domestic servants, human rights
abuses. By the mid-1970s women's organisations were well established
in the *peripheria* and were supported by the Catholic church and the
Marxist Left. The state initially tried to repress this flowering of
community-based political activity. Then, as the dictatorship's economic strategy created a chronic crisis and Brazil was increasingly

drawn into the IMF's structural adjustment net, the junta was forced into a form of controlled political liberalisation, involving the legalisation of political parties and the holding of parliamentary and presidential elections.

This macro analysis gives a broad-brush picture of developments in Brazil from the early 1960s to the early 1990s. A micro-political analysis reveals complexity layered upon complexity. So, for example, while the progressive shift in Catholicism in the 1960s (Vatican II, liberation theology, Christian base communities) brought material and ideological support to Brazilian women's organisations, churchmen's deep-seated essentialist view of women and patriarchal practices produced conflicts which at times undermined progressive political work. Similarly, interactions and alliances between working-class women and left-wing middle-class activists both supported and complicated the activities of women's organisations in the *peripheria*.

Case study analysis also reveals that community-based women's organisations were important emancipatory learning sites. In these organisations women were able to develop critical analyses of the material and ideological forces that shaped their lives. Over the twenty-five years that Alvarez examines, there was a growing recognition among women of the specificity of women's struggles and a clearer assertion of women's interests. There was also a growing recognition of the diversity of women's experiences and of a need for alliances based on a recognition of difference. There were also increasing complexities and difficulties as women's energies were drawn into electoral politics and struggles around state-sponsored policies.

What then can be said about learning and education in Brazilian women's movements during this period? Most obviously we can say that women's social movement activity had a learning dimension. But what exactly does this mean? Well, it means a number of things. Women's organisations and struggles constituted important *spaces* for learning. Learning requires time, and opportunity for discussion and reflection. Women's organisations provided these. *Critical* learning extends the learner, moves her beyond her current understanding. As we have seen, such learning developed in Brazilian women's organisations. *Emancipatory* learning involves learning generating emancipatory action. Again, this occurred in the Brazilian situation.

But exactly what is involved in critical and emancipatory learning?

How do learners move beyond their current understanding, and become motivated to act in emancipatory ways? Alvarez's reference to the importance of oppositional discourses in 'shaping the subjective possibilities' for political action is of interest here. Her study points to, but does not really develop an analysis of, the role of oppositional discourses in developing women's political consciousness and action in the 1960s, 1970s and 1980s. Yet there is sufficient data to enable us to begin to 'read in' such an analysis. (The following disussion is also informed by the first-person accounts of Brazilian women activists in Capiora Women's Group, 1993, and Puelo, 1994.)

The discourse of Brazilian women's movements was one of critique, demand and rights. The process by which this discourse was articulated and learned was one of participation in community-based organisations and campaigns. The core campaigns of women's organisations in the *peripheria* in the 1960s and 1970s, the cost of living and day-care campaigns, rested on a denunciation of miserable living conditions and made very clear political demands: for price freezes, day-care centres, and so forth. The campaigns employed mobilising and educative tactics like neighbourhood surveys and open letters, tactics which involved large numbers of people and educated them about both the issues and the forms of action. As these campaigns went on, the women involved in them became clearer about the nature of the state and its agents ('they lied to us') and how to deal with them ('If we're pressing them, things will happen').

What emerged in the neighbourhood struggles of Brazilian women in the 1960s and 1970s was an activist discourse, one which emphasised the importance of women acting on their own situations, and of them not being able to rely on others to act for them:

> If we leave it up to them we'll never get anything we need in the neighbourhood.

> We would go up there, fifteen or twenty or more of us, whenever we thought things were being held up.

This discourse was one of rights and demands. The rights that were demanded were those of women: 'as mothers we demanded a place to leave our children'. The process by which women learned to articulate these demands was gradual, sometimes torturous: 'Little by little we confirmed, in practice, the universality of certain sensations: the uneasiness or unrest of "being female", the feeling of suffering some injustice without exactly understanding its proportions.'

This discourse, too, was characterised by a growing awareness of the specificity of women's experience and oppression:

> Women suffer much more with problems of sex.
> Women also suffer a specific oppression because of the simple fact of being a woman.
> Women ... are ... doubly oppressed: as women and as a class.
> The women in our group did all the support work for the church but received no support for their own issues in return.

The discourse of Brazilian women's movements also encompassed a recognition of the universality and diversity of women's experience. While Brazilian women learned of the connections between them and of the importance of solidarity ('we cannot say goodbye now ... we must continue to struggle together'), they also learned of the diversity of their political experiences and ideologies and of the ways in which these differences could be exploited by men (as in the Jardim Miriam's women's group in the early 1980s, and in electoral politics).

From the 1960s to the 1980s, then, many Brazilian women acquired a sophisticated political discourse, one that helped them to understand the complexities of their situations and which empowered them to act against oppression. The acquisition of this discourse was for these women a radical, transformative learning experience. The experience of Brazilian women also shows that while emancipatory learning is cumulative and developmental, it is not linear, is embedded in conflict, and often develops in unanticipated ways. So, for example, Johnson and Johnson intended to sell sanitary napkins in Jardin Miriam, not to establish an activist women's organisation there. Ten years later, in the same neighbourhood, three middle-class organisers set out to establish a skills training course, not the discussion group which emerged in which women developed critical analysis and action around a range of issues.

Alvarez provides us with a very useful framework for analysing learning in social movements. Her data on Brazilian women's organisations suggest that encountering oppositional discourses is crucial in raising people's consciousness and preparing them for emancipatory action. In other words, the learning of these discourses provides a crucial bridge between the economic and political conditions that prepare the ground for social action, and the social action itself.

## Note

1.  A reader of the manuscript of this book correctly noted that there is a rich literature on the period of Brazilian history discussed in this chapter and that I could have drawn on it. I considered doing this when writing the chapter but in the end decided to focus my analysis on Alvarez's book, because it provides the rich contextual account of social movement activity that enables the 'reading in' of a learning dimension. While I have added a few references here, readers who wish to explore the Brazilian context in any depth are referred to Alvarez's extensive bibliography.

# CHAPTER 7

# Political Education in the Zimbabwe Liberation Struggle

## Liberation struggle and emancipatory learning

The case studies in this book give a picture of the complex dynamics of emancipatory learning in popular organisations, social action and workplaces. They also illustrate the difficulty of moving from local to broader struggles. The Brazilian chapter demonstrates this explicitly in its discussion of the negative effects of patriarchal practices on women's organisations, the problems of building a national women's movement and the complicated effects on women's organisations of the revival of electoral politics. But the difficulties of building a broad emancipatory political movement are implicit in the other studies. When so much effort goes into local struggles, and these struggles are so complex, there is little time and energy left for broader political work.

So how might people build a democratic and socialist politics beyond the local level? And what would be the role of learning and education in this process?

In the 1970s many of us on the Left saw struggles for national liberation in what was then referred to as the 'third world' as offering a model of large-scale democratic and socialist politics. Articulated in its classic form in China in the 1930s and 1940s, liberation struggle involved a relatively small, highly politicised group seeking to mobilise the mass of a population to overthrow an oppressive ruling class. Armed insurgency, democratic political work and systematic political education were central to the theory and practice of liberation struggle. Typically, liberation struggles were anti-imperialist and anti-capitalist, arising in colonial situations in which the coloniser refused to yield power. The instigators of liberation struggle were often educated people who had been frustrated in their attempts to negotiate a democratic transfer of political power. The refusal of the coloniser to negotiate left the colonised the alternatives of submission or armed insurgency. Insurgents quickly became reliant on the masses for their survival. Democratic, and in some cases, socialist relationships sometimes developed in the liberated zones of countries where armed struggle was being waged. At its best, liberation struggle generated a dialectic of cadres and masses which transformed feudal, capitalist and patriarchal relationships. (For discussion of the theory and practice of liberation struggle, see Cabral, 1973, 1974; Selden, 1973; Ross and Levy, 1989.)

To many on the western Left in the 1960s and 1970s it appeared that liberation struggle was a tidal wave which would roll over first the colonised world, and then the 'metropoles'. 'One, two, many Vietnams', Che Guevera pronounced. China, Cuba, Algeria, Vietnam, Mozambique, Angola: so the dominos teetered and fell. The student, anti-war, environmental and peace movements promised revolutionary change at the heart of capitalism. The Cultural Revolution in China promised a permanent revolution which would prevent the emergence of a new ruling class.

Today liberation struggle appears much less of an answer than it did twenty-five years ago. From the mid-1970s, there was a great reversal. Capitalism restructured, its dynamic centre shifting from Europe and North America to peripatetic corporations forever moving in search of cheap labour. Aggressive imperialism resurfaced, its vanguard an increasingly desperate United States beset by industrial decline and domestic unrest. The third world was bound by debt to the first, lacking the political will and means to break away. Eastern European state 'socialism' (in reality a form of welfare state capitalism) ground to a halt, brought down by the crippling arms expenditures of the long Cold War, western propaganda, and internal bureaucratic corruption and ossification. One by one the dominos were reincorporated into the global capitalist system (on these developments, see Chomsky, 1992, 1993; and Pilger, 1992). Liberation struggle now began to look like a passing phase, rather than the wave of the future. The focus of radical activity around the globe now became ways of building islands of democratic practice in a sea of capitalist domination, and making links between those islands.

To revisit liberation struggle in the light of this history is to see its complexities more clearly, and to redefine it. It is also to see the centrality of its learning dimension.

The examination of broader political struggles does not release us from complexity, ambiguity and contradiction. It compounds them. In this chapter, through an examination of the Zimbabwean experience, I argue that national liberation struggle is a contested social process with uncertain outcomes. I believe that it is only by recognising this that we can move away from the antithetical yet related fantasies of the inevitable triumph or failure of emancipatory movements. In the 1960s and 1970s many of us believed in the inexorable triumph of liberation struggle. We coopted the Right's domino theory, and cheered as each tile fell. Today, in the wake of the collapse of eastern European socialism, in an era of capitalist triumphalism, many on the Left have abandoned the possibility of socialism and have embraced a liberalism that assumes there is no alternative but to try to reform capitalism from within.

History scuttled the optimism of my generation; in time it will show the reformism of the current crop of left-liberals to be similarly illusionary. I will argue in this chapter that, like local struggles, national struggles are complex and contradictory. The struggle for liberation is not linear or developmental, nor is popular victory pre-ordained. And like local ones, national struggles demand sophisticated analysis if we are to learn from them.

This chapter traces connections within the Zimbabwe liberation struggle between learning and education, micro-politics and the national and global political economy. The particular issue addressed is whether, overall, political learning and education in the Zimbabwean national struggle promoted democracy and socialism, or whether they were too weak to counter the authoritarian political culture that was dominant in both the settler state and the nationalist movement. In discussing this issue, two dimensions of the relationship of education and liberation struggle are examined: the experience of colonialism as emancipatory education for the oppressed; and the systematic political education of cadres and masses in the latter phase of the national struggle.

## Context

From 1890 to 1980 the central African country of Zimbabwe was a white settler colony called Rhodesia. During these years a relatively small group of whites (numbering at their peak only a quarter of a million people, and outnumbered by Africans sixteen to one) controlled the economy and State. Half the country, containing the most productive agricultural land, was controlled by Europeans. Africans were relegated to scattered 'reserves', areas of poor farming land which by themselves could not support the African population. To survive, Africans were forced to sell their labour to whites for below-subsistence wages. In this distinctive system of exploitation the functioning of all institutions was shaped by the efforts of Europeans to maintain their economic and political domination.

African resistance to white exploitation was constant, and took various forms. By the late 1950s, Africans had formed their own political parties and were trying to persuade whites to share power. Such petitioning initially won some concessions. But in the early 1960s white determination to maintain political domination led to the formation of an unequivocally white supremacist party, the Rhodesian Front, which gained power in 1962, crushed open African political organisation, and in 1965 unilaterally declared its independence from Britain. Africans reacted by launching a guerrilla war, which began to have an effect from 1972. In 1978, in an attempt to stave off genuine majority rule, the Rhodesian Front reached an 'internal settlement' with minor African parties. This 'settlement' did not stop the guerrilla war, which increasingly took on the character of a socialist liberation struggle. At the end of 1979, fearful of the radicalising effects of the war on Zimbabwe politics, the British brokered peace talks between the internal settlement parties and the two major African nationalist parties. The latter, combined as the 'Patriotic Front', achieved power in full-franchise elections in March 1980 (Martin and Johnson, 1981; Foley, 1984a; Ranger, 1985).

## The development of political consciousness in the 1930s and 1940s

To understand organised nationalism we need to examine 'proto'-nationalism, the resistant consciousness and behaviour, much of it individualistic and indirect, that preceded and laid the foundations for organised African nationalism. In this section I will argue that the emergence of this proto-nationalism in Zimbabwe can be understood as vital and complex learning.

To be properly understood, learning and education must be located within their broader political and economic context. Throughout the colonial period, for most Zimbabweans there was one overriding fact of existence: they had a subordinate position in the colonial political economy. Until the late 1950s, African politics in Rhodesia was still largely accommodationist – Africans were still trying to persuade white settlers to share power and wealth. But from the 1930s we can detect a sharper African political consciousness developing. In that decade the first national newspaper for black Zimbabweans appeared. Published in Bulawayo, with articles in English and African languages, the *Bantu Mirror* was initially under the control of the Native Affairs Department. On 5 February 1938, the leading article in the paper was headed 'What will be the future of Native Education in this country?' It was written by L. M. Sebetso, and began:

> One of the paramount features of Native education is in the feeling among certain Europeans that it is their imperative duty to retain their status of superiority and dominance if they are to evade being swamped both socially and economically by the educated Natives ...
>
> Native education, it is feared, will swell the number of claimants for the franchise, encourage miscegenation and reduce the number of farm labourers. It is quite obvious that these arguments are directed by a fear complex.
>
> It is a natural thing for a Native to feel dissatisfied. ... He wishes to be regarded as a constituent part of the Southern Rhodesia democracy. He wants a voice in the affairs of the country in which he lives, pays taxes and has to obey the laws. He wants fair and impartial educational facilities. History teaches us that the movement for national liberty in all European countries in the 18th and 19th centuries was due to the fact that parliaments were represented by a very small section of the people, had no education policy, and all Governments were in the hands of small, almost hereditary groups. This state of affairs brought about the opposition of the unprivileged classes. At present the Natives lack liberal education. (Sebetso, 1938: 1, 10)

In this letter the writer identifies the economic, political and psychological bases of the settler state's segregationist policies. He also demands, rather than pleas for, political and educational equality, supporting his demands by referring to historical precedent – in particular, the popular struggle for political democracy in Europe – and through reference to universal ethical principles ('fair and impartial'). His argument is in part an appeal to reason ('It is a natural thing for a Native to feel dissatisfied ... ') and in part critical, in the sense that the writer seeks to expose the hidden dynamic of European domination – white fear of being overwhelmed economically and politically by Africans. In the rest of his letter, Sebetso develops a case for equality of educational opportunity for Africans, again couching his argument in nationalistic terms ('There is no reason why African education should be different from the one given in European schools ... ') and referring to other popular movements ('The world has become one and its movements are influencing Native life tremendously ... '). His language is one of critique and demand, not petition.

Sebetso's article initiated a significant debate about education in the pages of the *Bantu Mirror*, a debate that drew in the highest echelons of the settler state. Three weeks after Sebetso's article appeared, the editor of the *Bantu Mirror* wrote a detailed rejoinder, in which he restated the segregationist state's ideology. The reason for this rebuttal was made clear. 'We recently', the editor wrote, 'had to visit the Prime Minister on a business matter. We found him engaged reading Mr. Sebetso's article. ... The purpose of the visit was for the time forgotten in discussing the article' (*Bantu Mirror*, 26/2/1938: 4). The editor's intervention generated many letters from African correspondents, most in support of Sebetso and employing the same discourse of reason, rights and demand (for discussion of these letters, see Foley, 1981: 50–3).

Despite the emerging political assertiveness found in these letters, in the 1930s the political consciousness of educated Africans was ambiguous and frequently contradictory.[1] Alongside the indications of a growing awareness of the economic and political sources of exploitation and oppression there was plenty of evidence of a colonised consciousness, the latter being a measure of the ideological distortions which had to be overcome before the nationalist movement could act effectively.

The theme of many letters and articles in the *Bantu Mirror* during this period was that African problems were attributable to African 'backwardness' and that the answer was to educate Africans to spread 'civilisation' to their people. These letters were often elitist and denigrated the majority of Africans. There were frequent references to 'natives', and a distinction was often made between the 'educated' and 'barbarians' or 'uncivilised people'. The letters also demonstrated a blind faith in technical solutions to social problems, and an equally blind faith in an evolutionary, Eurocentric notion of 'progress'. 'Civilisation' was seen by many Africans as European, and as being transmitted by Europeans to Africans, who should be grateful for it (*Bantu Mirror*, 26/2/1938: 4).

Such thinking mystified the social sources of exploitation and oppression. But it was not simply, as some scholars have argued, a manifestation of Africans' 'self-denigration and gratitude to the white elite, and a sign of their acceptance of the unequal and repressive social order' (Kinloch, 1974: 71—2). There was more to it than that. For Zimbabwean Africans, the 1920s and 1930s were a period of learning. They were learning the importance, and difficulty, of organised self-help in an exceptionally oppressive and exploitative political economy. The reliance on, and expressions of gratitude to, Europeans were transitory phenomena. As Africans acquired political skills, and in doing so came to understand more clearly the nature of the struggle in which they were involved, the expressions of gratitude and submissiveness gave way to anger and assertiveness. 'Your policy' wrote Charles Mzingeli, the secretary of the first African trade union in Zimbabwe, the Industrial and Commercial Workers Union, to the Rhodesian Prime Minister in 1933, 'is to teach Africans 100 per cent respect for white men and your policy is to deprive Africans of their privileges to organise themselves for their advancement ... ' (Letter from Charles Mzingeli to the Editor, *Rhodesian Weekly Review*, 12/9/33, in NAZ S1542/C16: *Complaints: Native, June 1933–December 1934*.).[2]

By the late 1940s much of the ambiguity – the mixture of assertion and subservience that had characterised African political consciousness in the earlier colonial period had gone. There was now a straightforward rejection of ideologies that rationalised the exploitation of Africans. This sharpening political consciousness was grounded in deteriorating living conditions in the rural areas and the creation of an urban working class. The loosening of ties between Zimbabwe and Britain because of World War Two enabled a degree of industrialisation in Zimbabwe, which in turn brought with it the need to attract a stable African workforce. At the same time the Reserves were becoming increasingly unable to provide a living for African families. The first half of the 1940s also saw a growing inability of urban African wages to meet the cost of living. The declining value of wages, together with the refusal of most white employers to grant wage rises, radicalised the urban working class and led to a series of strikes (Foley, 1984a: 446–54).

A reading of African newspapers and the minutes of African organisations reveals a sharpening of political consciousness in the late 1940s. There was a variety of political expression and a burgeoning of political and quasi-political activity, including a new growth of separatist churches. The government was lobbied about improving urban living conditions for Africans and other issues (Foley, 1984a: 455). Demands were made for better race relations and an end to segregation (Andrewson, 1949).

Two themes characterise the African political discourse of this period: increasingly acute analyses of the nature of the colonial political economy, and a developing awareness of the need for political organisation. A 1949 letter to the *Bantu Mirror* combined these themes. Beginning with a critique of the Rhodesian system of land apportionment, which reserved the most 'fertile and healthy' land for whites and increasingly rendered Africans 'landless and homeless', the writer went on to argue that 'Africans cannot stand against this organised world if they themselves are not organised'. What was needed is a national African political organisation (Mtmkulu, 1949. For further analysis of the development of African political thinking in the 1940s, see Foley, 1984a: 458–74.)

## The shift to armed struggle

The style of African nationalist politics that developed in Zimbabwe was shaped by the nature of the settler state. For many years, any attempt at political organisation by Zimbabweans which might have led to a redistribution of power was carefully monitored or quickly repressed by the government. Then, from the mid-1950s African nationalist organisations began to form. Even though these organisations were generally moderate in their demands, their activities and the growing militancy of nationalist organisations in other African countries, particularly in neighbouring Nyasaland (now Malawi) and Northern Rhodesia (now Zambia), panicked Southern

Rhodesian whites and led to the banning of African political parties, the declaration of a state of emergency and a spate of repressive legislation which all but eliminated the notion of the rule of law in Zimbabwe.

This repression drove the nationalist organisations to more confrontationist tactics – strikes, boycotts, riots, destruction of property (see, for example, Foley, 1993b). The election of the white supremacist Rhodesian Front government in 1962 made increasingly untenable the position of those black rationalists who still hoped for a negotiated end to minority rule. A fierce debate over tactics was waged in the main nationalist party, the Zimbabwe African People's Union (ZAPU), throughout 1962 and 1963. One outcome of this debate was the formation in 1963 of a new nationalist party, the Zimbabwe African National Union (ZANU) by Nadabaningi Sithole, Robert Mugabe and other prominent leaders. ZANU immediately began to send cadres to China, and later to Cuba, for guerrilla training. ZAPU also soon began to send cadres for training – to China, and later, and in greater numbers, to the Soviet Union and Cuba (Foley, 1993d: 478—84).

From 1964 onwards both ZAPU and ZANU infiltrated considerable numbers of fighters into Zimbabwe. As they were not informed by a developed political strategy, these early incursions were easily contained by the settler forces. This phase of the armed struggle tapered off in 1967 and 1968 when guerrillas suffered heavy casualties in conventional battles with the Rhodesian army. From then until the end of 1972 there was little fighting in Zimbabwe as both black nationalist parties formulated a new approach to armed struggle. Positional warfare aimed at achieving an immediate transfer of power was abandoned in favour of a gradual infiltration of guerrillas who would engage in military operations only after winning the political support of the people. This strategy was effective in limiting the exercise of state power in rural areas, and also caused a decline in agricultural production.

The coming to power of a Marxist government in Mozambique in 1975 raised the prospect of increased guerrilla activity in Zimbabwe and the eventual accession to power of a Marxist government there. This prompted Britain, the United States and South Africa to try to construct a 'settlement' which would lead to the installation of a 'moderate' African government in Zimbabwe. This took another five years. In February 1980 the nominally Marxist Patriotic Front won an overwhelming majority in the first universal franchise election in Zimbabwe's history. The Patriotic Front soon abandoned any real radicalism and settled down to ruling on behalf of the privileged classes (Foley, 1982; Moore, 1991).

Why, after ninety years of struggle against colonialism, including nearly a decade of guerrilla war that linked military strategy to the building of democracy and socialism, was independent Zimbabwe so readily re-incorporated into global capitalism? In what follows, I will argue that the answer lies in an understanding of the interrelationship of three factors – the Zimbabwe political economy, the micro-politics of the liberation movements, and the nature of political learning and education in the liberation struggle in the 1960s and 1970s.

## Political learning and education during the early phase of armed struggle

As noted above, from the early 1960s both ZANU and ZAPU sent young Zimbabweans to socialist countries for military training. Despite differences in orientation in the training offered by different socialist countries, all the training was fundamentally political. Samuel Kikubi, a ZIPRA[3] cadre who trained in the Soviet Union in 1968, recalls that political education there focused on

> the exploitative nature of capitalism, ... imperialism and classes obtaining ... in the colonies, how these dominant classes relate with the externally based bourgeois classes. ... [This education] concentrated on ... how to transform that capitalist system into a socialist system, with the emphasis on the leadership of the working class. ... And in peasant-dominated countries the necessity of the working class to form an alliance with the peasantry in order to overthrow an exploitative regime ...[4]

Instruction in Russia lasted 'about a year'. Reading focused on 'the fundamental principles of Marxism-Leninism'. Works read included Lenin's *Alliance of Workers and Peasants*, *The Communist Manifesto*, 'and we did read a bit about Mao Tse-Tung's military writings'. Methods of instruction largely consisted of direct lecturing. But there was 'quite a lot of discussion' in each class and one day a week there was a two-hour seminar. Each trainee was supposed to prepare something for these seminars and one or two people would lead the discussion. The subject matter of the seminars was the lessons of the previous week and specifically the application of the theory of these lessons to the Zimbabwean situation.

This kind of analysis was anathema to the older nationalist leaders, who told the recruits to concentrate on the military training and to 'forget about Marxism, that's theirs, it's not ours'. But the opposition of the political leaders did not stop some cadres applying the historical materialist theory they had acquired to their own situation. By the end of the fourth month of training in Russia

> we began to ask ourselves, when we had gone deep into the problem of capitalism, ... we began to say 'Really, do we want to work in order to enrich other people at our own expense? Is this what we are fighting for? If our leaders say we shouldn't worry about Marxism, should we accept that? ... ' Of course at first we disagreed. But by the end of the sixth month we all agreed that the leaders were wrong.

The recruits were also inspired by the student and worker movements of the late 1960s in western Europe. 'The challenge of capitalism by people within the capitalist states themselves' helped the recruits to agree that 'capitalism must go, even in our country'.

Asked how trainees had related the theory they were taught in Russia to the Zimbabwean situation, Kikubi said that they had recognised that there was 'a capitalist system in the country ... based on profit making ... , and most of these profits are repatriated to the metropolitan countries'. This insight caused the recruits to question the value of achieving independence

> without changing the system of production which still allows the profits to go to individuals ... [and] very large companies, in fact monopolies, which are based outside the country. How to change this for the benefit of the people? If we allow it, is it not just removing a white man from power and replacing him with a black man without changing the system of exploitation?

Back in the ZIPRA camps in Zambia a struggle over the nature of political education took place between politicians and fighters. The guerrillas wanted the formalisation of political teaching. Within ZIPRA every detachment had a political commissar. Decisions about the content of political education were supposed to be taken by the chief political commissar, who was aligned with the political leadership. Political instruction in the camps transmitted a nationalist view of history which emphasised the venerableness of indigenous cultures and political systems and their destruction by European colonialism, but was silent on the nature of the colonial and global political economy. 'Nothing was said about the ... forces that controlled the system of production ... and the social structure of the oppressed was not ... analysed at all.' Kikubi did not encounter this sort of historical materialist analysis in official ZAPU discourse until 'I was in Britain in the seventies [and] I read something in the *Zimbabwe Review* [a ZAPU journal published in London] where the multi-national corporations were thoroughly analysed by someone. ... But even then here was a note by the editor, who happened to be member of the [ZAPU] Central Committee, who said the views expressed here don't necessarily represent those of the party.' For Kikubi and his comrades 'that was devastating, it was just conclusive that ZAPU was not committed officially towards transforming this country into a socialist country, never'.

But in the Zambian camps in the late 1960s and early 1970s political commissars who had been trained overseas still found opportunities to insert Marxist concepts into their teaching, especially in sessions on economic issues. 'There most of the commissars did not have any notes from headquarters and they took their own initiative. They drew on what they had learned in Russia and Cuba. And also ZAPU allowed a lot of Marxist literature to come in and the commissars controlled it.' Guerrillas were free to borrow this material from the camp library.

## The struggle within the struggle

By the late 1960s large numbers of ZAPU guerrillas were being 'infiltrated into the country and being caught before they did anything'. Kikubi remembers this strategy as having failed 'because people tried to act militarily ... without mobilising the people'. The older, more conventional, nationalist leaders 'just took for granted' that the political work done inside Zimbabwe in the early 1960s, which had focused on organising public rallies and neighbourhood party cells in the urban areas, 'had done their work ... and were enough to keep [the people's] consciousness in progress'. But the guerrillas' experience of war in the rural areas of Zimbabwe was showing that this strategy was ill-founded. This in turn generated a protracted struggle between the fighters and the old-guard ZAPU leaders. This conflict came to a head when ZAPU guerrillas arrested most of the party's Central Committee and asked the Zambian Government to arbitrate the dispute over military strategy. But the Zambians, while pretending to be sympathetic to the guerrillas, connived with the ZAPU leadership to disarm the fighters. The forty-odd, most politically sophisticated guerrillas were weeded out and provided scholarships to Britain, where they sat out the rest of the war! By removing the most politically advanced guerrillas from the struggle, the Zambians and the ZAPU old-guard leaders ensured that progressive, mobilising and transforming styles of work rarely developed in areas controlled by ZAPU during the liberation struggle.[5]

ZANU was more successful than ZAPU in developing a mass-based style of work. Its ability to do this may be largely attributable to its area of greatest popular support being in eastern Zimbabwe, where ZANU was able to establish a secure base with the support of Frelimo, the Mozambique liberation movement which came to government in 1975. The relatively (in comparison with ZAPU) progressive nature of the ZANU leadership may have been another factor (Nyagumbo, 1980; Sithole, n.d.; Smith, et al., 1981). ZANU conducted systematic political education in eastern Zimbabwe from the early 1970s, playing on popular grievances over taxes and land. Increasingly, the countryside became safe for the guerrillas and unsafe for the Rhodesian army. By the late 1970s ZANLA was engaging Rhodesian troops in positional warfare and conducting raids in major urban areas (Meredith, 1979; Martin and Johnson, 1981: 26–8, 73).

Despite ZANU's military and political successes, intra-party conflicts and international pressures limited its effectiveness as a liberation movement. In the mid-1970s a series of struggles between guerrillas and politicians, similar in nature to those that had destroyed ZIPRA's combat effectiveness, wracked ZANU. As in ZAPU, ZANU guerrillas rebelled against their political leaders and were, with the help of the front-line states, outmanoeuvred by them. Politically, radical ZANU fighters were disarmed and gaoled, and in some instances murdered. The war was disrupted, conventional politicians gained control of ZANLA and worked with the front-line states, Britain, the United States and South Africa to put in place an agreement which brought ZANU and ZAPU together in the Patriotic Front and which subsequently saw the conventional politicians win the independence elections of February 1980. (Foley, 1984b).

## Political education within the liberation movements in the 1970s

The triumph of the conventional politicians affected the character of political education in the liberation movements. Interviews with former ZANLA fighters who trained in Mozambique from 1975 onwards suggest that the instruction was largely military. Military training consisted of instruction in the use of weapons, daily drilling and 'a lot of running'. In both ZANU and ZAPU political education tended to be restricted to people with high school education or above. The ZANU leadership saw the large numbers of school students who ran away from school and joined the struggle from 1975 onwards as potential cadres. The assumption was that 'educated' recruits would be able to absorb party ideology and transmit it to the peasantry, who were believed to be unable to absorb it without such help (Interviews 1 and 4;[6] speech by Zimbabwe Minister of Labour, Mr Kangai, Inaugural Seminar of Zimbabwe Institute of Development Studies, Harare, 30/3/82).

Another factor influencing the kind of instruction recruits were getting in the second half of the 1970s was the huge number of people who joined up. As the number of recruits increased, the amount of instruction most of them received decreased. The only training a recruit who joined ZIPRA in 1977 received was three weeks orientation. This consisted of instruction in 'self-defence', and political training for an hour a day. The latter focused on 'the style of government which the black people would like to see ... a bit of ... [a] socialist government', a social system in which profits would be shared by producers and cooperative farms would be encouraged. Even for 'educated' recruits, political instruction in the ZANU camps was sporadic. There was no regular timetable of political instruction, which occurred 'sometimes once a week, or once a month'. 'At the rear (in the Mozambique camps) most of our time was spent constantly constructing things' (Interviews 2 and 4).

Despite the sporadic nature of their training, former guerrillas interviewed in 1982 could still recall the substance of the political education they received in the camps. In their political orientation in the Mozambique camps recruits were given four basic lessons. The first was called, 'The Grievances of the Masses' and it consisted of an analysis of the grievances of 'the broad masses' and the 'imperialist government's' failure to respond to them. The second lesson, called 'The People's Army' instructed recruits in the proper behaviour of soldiers in a liberation army. Recruits were told they were expected to do political and productive work as well as fight. The third lesson looked at how soldiers were to work with the people – 'how to approach the masses, how you've got to mobilise the masses and ... how you've got to treat the masses ... '. The fourth lesson was about the party and its ideology, and focused on the issues of how ZANU–PF[7] had adopted armed struggle, the main aims of the party, and the good things that would result from the struggle (Interview 1).

The themes of political education for ZANLA cadres were: the history of colonial oppression, the need for solidarity and sacrifice in the struggle, the history of ZANU and the theory of guerrilla war. Interviewees' clearest recollections were of theoretical and experiential learning about the importance of unity, and about the need to create a symbiosis of fighters and people (Interviews 2, 5, 6). As one former ZANLA fighter put it:

> They said, you should work hand in hand with the people, because the people ... were said to be, I don't know what word I can use, ... in Shona ... it ... means ... 'Without the people the guerrilla movement should have not succeeded'. So it depended upon the masses. They were the people who told us everything about the enemy's troops, then they were the people who fed us, and they were the people who gave us protection from those rains which were falling during the struggles ... they were the people who gave us blankets and all the supplies depended on them. We carried nothing from Mozambique, you just came carrying a rifle and your ammunition, that's all ... (Interviews 1, 5 and 6)

In guerrilla political education the notion of exploitation tended to be conceived in racial terms. Asked what he understood by exploitation, a former ZIPRA guerrilla said:

> By this I rather say it is whereby the other race is felt [to be] inferior, it is looked at as if it's inferior to the other one, and the opportunities in jobs and many other things, posts and what have you, were granted to the other, were just too rare to Africans, these were granted to the other race. (Interview 4)

This racial conception of exploitation was fostered by mass and cadre education which focused on the white conquest of Zimbabwe and the system of exploitation which grew out of it. But cadre education in this period, at least in ZANLA, seems to have fostered some understanding of the notions of class, class exploitation and capitalism. One recruit had learned that 'there's not much difference between the working class and the peasants, ... [both] these classes are exploited'. Another guerrilla learned that

> there's a capitalist system whereby the rich man gets, becomes, richer and richer by exploiting the poor man. ... For instance .. when I buy a wheelbarrow. In this area where I am staying there is no [one] with a wheelbarrow. And if you want to use my wheelbarrow ... . you have to give me some cash for it. ... And in the end you find I will get a lot of money and to buy more wheelbarrows and maybe end up buying buses and so forth. And you might find that now I'm in love with money and not with say, with the well-being of the people. ... In this way I'm always exploiting people because of my love for money you see. I'm getting richer and richer! And these are the things we tried to show ... the people, that these things are a disadvantage to them. Why is it that there are some people who are very rich and some people who are very poor. We were trying to tell them that, and the only way to kind of solve this problem as we saw it was this communal way of living ... (Interviews 5 and 6)

Here the concept of exploitation moves past being a racial notion. Anyone who puts money before people is seen as an exploiter. The seeds of the Marxist notion of exploitation as the extraction of surplus labour is also present, as is the idea of having to change relations of production to end exploitation: 'the only way to ... solve this problem ... was this communal way of living'.

It seems that the political education received by most guerrillas in the later phase of the liberation war equipped them with some historical materialist concepts but was insufficient to develop in them a coherent Marxist theory and practice. It is also likely that only those cadres who received systematic and prolonged political instruction early in the liberation war, and who had considerable experience of armed and political struggle, were able to develop a sophisticated political analysis. It is not yet clear how many of these people there were, or what was the precise nature of their politics. But it is clear that the rapid expansion of guerrilla numbers in the mid-1970s itself ensured that experienced cadres were in the minority. Further, as we have seen, in both ZANU and ZAPU, cadres who wanted to develop a more deeply Marxist theory and practice were purged. These factors combined to ensure that both parties remained firmly in the hands of leaders oriented to a much more conventional politics. The hegemony of these leaders did much to determine the trajectory of post-independence politics and economic policy. This interpretation is suggested both by these interviews and by Moore's (1991: 488–95) review of the debate about the 'struggle within the struggle'.

## Mass political education and learning in the later stages of the liberation struggle

Despite these developments it appears that during the 1970s, in some parts of the country at least, ZANU developed a democratic and empathetic way of working with the people. Three political scientists who examined the structures built up by ZANU among the people during the war concluded that four levels of organisation had been established, at the village, ward, district and provincial levels. These committees 'dealt with everything concerning the war'. 'Grass roots village committees dealt with day-to-day problems of feeding and clothing the guerillas and basic services to the community. But issues concerning the outlay of large sums of money, for example, would be passed on to a higher committee.' In some places 'the Rhodesian state apparatuses had been excluded' and 'the committee structure was on the way to becoming an alternative administration. While there was no widespread restructuring of production, the committees did provide the impetus for some self-help.' However, the researchers concluded that because of the nature of the war – colonial forces in apparent control of the countryside during the day, guerrillas in control at night – few liberated zones developed in Zimbabwe. The Zimbabwe liberation movements were, in the main, more effective in destroying the settler economy and administration than in establishing their own alterative structures (Cliffe et al., 1980: 49–57; *Rhodesian Herald*, 27/7/74).

One of the achievements of ZANLA's political work was the psychological affinity it created between cadres and people. The main instrument of mass political education was the *pungwe*, the local political gathering, which involved not only political lectures given by cadres but also a large measure of participation through the means of *chimurenga* (liberation war) songs and slogans. *Pungwe* would be held at a 'GP', a gathering point, a house or a clearing in the bush, where people would assemble after the evening meal. The messages that were reiterated over and over at *pungwe* were the importance of unity and self-reliance among the people. Probably the most frequently heard slogan at these meetings was, 'We are our own liberators by direct confrontation'. A *pungwe* would typically open with party slogans lionising the Mugabe faction of ZANU and denigrating its political oponents (Interviews 1, 5 and 6; Cliffe et al., 1980: 52—4).

A Catholic priest present at numerous *pungwe*s recalls that guerrillas continually raised four issues: 'One is land. The other is education. The other is sharing in industry and so on and the means of production. And the other one, ... is the closure of the gap in wages' (Interview 7). Another Catholic priest gave the following description of political work in the Midlands in 1977:

> They teach their catechism by rote and song. Freedom songs make the rounds at beer drinks in the evenings when the mood is festive, thus creating a feeling of freedom. Essentially, they state that they will reclaim the land of their forefathers, led – as they claim to be – by their ancestral spirits. The movement is thus given a distinctly religious line that leads right back to the first Shona rebellion [in 1890]. The riches of the land, mines and plantations belong to all and not merely to few whites. (Cited in Linden, 1980: 248)

Guerrillas also instructed the people in the benefits of collective work:

> And we would ... cite a number of situations where this communal life has been an advantage to the masses. And we had some, say, small magazines from China, from Russia, and these would show some farmers who were working together and some industrial people working together ... [8]

> And we could also give examples, for instance, they knew the [aspirant ZANU] government want[ed] to give tractors to the farmers. It cannot afford to give ... a tractor to each farmer. But they [the people] have got to unite in small villages in a small number. Then they could be given a tractor and they then share, and things like that. And when building dams and water supply pipes, you should be collectivised, that is a system of staying together so that the Ministry of Water Development ... can supply them with water and pipes and even electricity.[9]

ZANLA's mass political work created a solid popular base for armed struggle, and it ensured ZANU's overwhelming victory in the 1980 election. But in the final phase of the war political education was nationalist, not socialist. In the main, it focused on the need to end colonial oppression by electing a popular government rather than on the importance of transforming production relations. According to one of the priests I interviewed in 1982, the guerrillas' political instruction was not very 'nuanced'. It transmitted a 'very simple idea of socialism, that we'll share all these goods ... when the thing is over'. The idea of class 'was played down because the racial issue was so big that you didn't need the kind of Marxist thing about the class struggle really. ... The class struggle was here identified as the race struggle' (Interview 7).

According to this priest, ZANLA's political work had begun to transform the people's consciousness, enabling them to shrug off the negative

> stereotypes that the Europeans had provided for them saying that they were ... illiterate, that they had no kind of real aptitude for skills, that they were in fact a people who couldn't reach the same kind of know-how as Europeans. And by constantly being kicked and downtrodden the people had accepted to a very great extent, maybe unconsciously ... the kind of idea the Europeans had given them of themselves. ... I would say to some extent they had an inferiority complex. Now this is one thing the guerrilla education during the war cleared up. The people became more self-confident and more critical, in the sense that Paulo Freire would say they became more aware of the kind of fatalism they had, and what they could do by their own initiatives and by their own ... gifts and skills.
>
> And so we had this uplifting of the people and this made a big difference when it came to the elections. We had the people then who had turned completely against the Europeans now becoming aware of how much they had lost, and aware of what they could achieve if they pulled together. (Interview 7)

ZANLA's mass political education enabled people to reject colonialism and it prepared them to vote for a particular party in the independence election. But it did not give the peasantry attitudes and skills that would enable them to participate in transforming the unequal and oppressive society that was Zimbabwe's inheritance at independence. Political instruction recruited the peasantry for ZANU rather than mobilising it for socialism. The same point can be made about the political education of the majority of guerrillas.

A clearer understanding of the processes that generated this outcome awaits further research. But it is clear that a major determinant of the political education that ZANLA gave both its own cadres and the people was the continued domination of ZANU by a leadership that was interested in capturing state power rather than in transforming society. This meant that the dominant political discourse in the vital latter phase of the liberation struggle emphasised the racial nature of colonialism, de-emphasised class and legitimised the old-guard leadership of ZANU. The explanation for this emphasis lies in the micro-politics of the Zimbabwe liberation movements and broader political and economic influences. In both major nationalist parties guerrillas who had learned a Marxist discourse and conventional political leaders who were hostile to this discourse vied for control; in both parties the latter emerged triumphant. Their victory coincided with the desire of the United States, Britain and South Africa to prevent a Marxist government coming to power. So both micro-political factors and a broader geo-political agenda converged to bring about a settlement of the 'Rhodesian question', and in this process political learning and education in the armed struggle played an important, and ultimately conservative, role. Support for this thesis is provided by other research on the later phase of the liberation struggle and by the development, in post-independence Zimbabwe, of a form of neo-colonial capitalism, presided over by an emerging black ruling class (Mubako, 1976; Foley, 1978, 1982; Meredith, 1979; Sithole, n.d.; Cliffe et al., 1980; Linden, 1980; Nyagumbo, 1980; Martin and Johnson, 1981; Smith et al., 1981; Ranger, 1985; Moore, 1991).

## Notes

1. 'Educated' here means 'educated in school'. 'Schooled' would be a more appropriate word.

2. Mzingeli sent a copy of his letter to the Prime Minister, with a covering letter, and was told by the Chief Native Commissioner that his proper channel for approaching the Prime Minister was through the Chief Native Commissioner 'a fact of which you have been informed on many occasions'. CNC to Mzingeli, 28/9/33, in S1542/C16, op. cit. For further evidence of African assertiveness in this period, see Foley, 1984a: 336–9.

3. ZIPRA is the acronym for the Zimbabwe People's Revolutionary Army, the military wing of ZAPU.

4. Interview with 'Samuel Kikubi' (a pseudonym), Harare, 17/3/82 and 23/4/82. This section is based on this interview.

5. This paragraph is a greatly condensed summary of Kikubi's detailed account of the struggle within ZAPU. The circumstances surrounding

Kikubi's account are supported by other evidence – see, for example, Mubako, 1976: especially 44–6, 48–58; Martin and Johnson, 1981: 13, 29–31, 215–23; and Moore, 1991: 488–95.

6. In 1982 I interviewed a number of former guerrillas and *mujibas* (messengers for guerrillas). Some of these former combatants were so young that they were able to go back to school after the war. Most of the interviews were done at schools. For brevity, I will only cite the interview numbers in the text.

7. ZANU–PF was the majority faction of ZANU, led by Robert Mugabe, which combined with ZAPU to form the Patriotic Front in 1976. ZANU–PF was opposed by a minority faction of the party, led by Ndabaningi Sithole.

8. Interview 5.

9. Interview 6.

CHAPTER 8
. . . . . . . . . . .
# Conclusion

I begin this Conclusion by discussing how I use the analysis developed in the book in work with adult and popular educators. I then review the theoretical framework of the book, and relate it to a broader body of adult education theory. Finally, I consider the implications of the analysis for future research and action.

## Application

In a popular education workshop I was involved in recently, an activist from a South East Asian country spoke of the practical importance of theory. For the past several years he and several of his colleagues had conducted a discussion group, built around reading theorists like Raymond Williams, Louis Athusser and Michel Foucault. Such reading, the activist said, enabled him and his colleagues both to develop their understanding of the broader political and economic forces that determined their work, and to become clearer about their own theoretical and political assumptions. He spoke passionately about the need for theory that both explains and enables action.

This book was written with precisely these ends in mind. I have found that the theoretical framework developed in the book can be of use to adult educators and activists working in community-based, social movement, institutional and even corporate settings. This framework encourages people to recognise that

- learning is a dimension of human life and manifests itself in many forms;
- education and learning are shaped by economic and political forces beyond participants' immediate influence;

- emancipatory learning and education are possible, but are also complex, ambiguous and continually contested;
- it is both possible and necessary to develop an analysis of this complexity and to act strategically. (For more on this last point, see Foley, 1995b: Chapter 1.)

In using this framework in sessions with educators and activists, I work from participants' experience and use case study material which enables people to develop a picture of the detailed dynamics of learning in struggle. Sessions begin with a discussion of participants' work contexts and concerns, elicited through a focus question such as: 'What aspects of the context of your work currently most concern you?' Participants discuss the focus question in pairs and small groups. We then discuss the broad conception of adult learning and education, and the framework for analysing learning and struggle outlined in the Introduction to this book (pp. 1–13). The introduction of this conceptual material is accompanied by small group discussion of examples drawn from participants' experience. Using overhead transparencies, I then draw on the case study material in this book to present a detailed analysis of learning in struggle. In each case study we examine the macro-economic and political context, the micro-politics, the overall pattern of learning, and the relationship of ideology, discourse and learning. For example, we study the clash between the professional and activist discourses in the campaign to reopen the gynaecological clinic (pp. 17–20). In discussing the Terania Creek campaign, we examine the forms of learning summarised in the table (pp. 40–5), and identify three central tensions in the campaign (production versus environment, experts versus activists, bureaucratic representative democracy versus direct democracy). With the neighbourhood house, Brazilian and Zimbabwean studies we spend time analysing excerpts from interviews for what they tell us about what and how people learned in these struggles. Analysis of the case study material leads to discussion of examples drawn from the participants' experience, and of the practical implications of the analysis.

## Theory

The theme of this book is learning in emancipatory struggle. In the theoretical framework developed in the book, learning and education are seen as complex and contested social activities. I suggest that to develop a picture of this complexity one needs to write case studies of learning in struggle, making explanatory connections between the broad political and economic context, micro-politics, ideologies, discourses and learning. The theoretical position I adopt is a straightforwardly historical materialist one.

A 'contestation' framework provides the theoretical underpinning of the book. Initially stated in the Introduction and elaborated upon in Chapter 4, this framework rests on the assumptions that domination and resistance to it are universal, and that while domination has an ideological dimension, it originates in economic and political relationships. The implications of this position are spelt out most fully in Chapter 5. The behaviour, learning and consciousness of the miners discussed in this chapter is, however much it may be mediated by other factors like attachment to family and community, ultimately determined by their place in the capitalist production process. Their essential experience of this process is of having their labour exploited. This exploitation occurs in a particular way, with management rather crudely and clumsily trying to squeeze more out of workers and workers recognising these attempts and resisting them with determination and humour. The workers' enjoyment of the struggle, while admirable and politically significant, should not divert us from understanding its nature. It is managers trying to extract the surplus labour of workers and workers resisting this. It is class struggle, in capitalism.

The set of theoretical constructs and political concerns which are the foundation of this book are very different from those of mainstream Anglo-American adult education theory which, as noted in the Introduction, focuses on decontextualised individual learners, educational technique and course provision. In recent years there has been much, justifiable, criticism of the instrumental and 'soft humanist' character of this body of theory (see, for example, Welton, 1987a, 1991; Bright, 1989; Collard and Law, 1989; Usher and Bryant, 1989; Hart, 1990b, 1992; Clark and Wilson, 1991; Collins, 1991).[1] But much of this recent critical adult education theory has itself manifested some of the problems of the 'mainstream' work that it criticises. This newer work often tends to the abstract, the epistemological, the psychological or the individualistic (for a discussion of this, see Foley, 1993a, 22). It is also often overly concerned with debates among professionals, rather than with working out ways of connecting adult education with struggles for social justice (for an example of this tendency see CPAE, 1991).

There are some notable exceptions to this, which together constitute an alternative corpus of adult education scholarship. The work of Gelpi (1979, 1985; see also Ireland, 1979) is informed by Marxist political economy. Frank Youngman's (1986) book is a sustained attempt to develop an historical materialist analysis of adult education, and his and Paul Wangoola's edited collection of papers (Wangoola and Youngman, 1996) is a pioneering contribution to the development of a political economy of adult education. The 1992 Conference of the Canadian Association for the Study of Adult Education held a series of symposia on the political economy of adult education, focusing on the restructuring, in the interests of capital, of economy, workplace and adult education (Taylor and Bedard 1992; Thomson, 1993: 96–7), and there have been a trickle of articles and book chapters on this theme (Foley, 1992, 1994, 1995b; Dunk et al., 1996; Brown, 1997, 1999). Peter Mayo's work on Gramsci and Freire, in a series of articles (1993, 1994, 1995, 1996, 1997; Allman and Mayo, 1997) and in his book (1998), demonstrates the capacity of historical materialism to blend economic, political and cultural analysis in ways which illuminate – and give strategic direction to – adult education practice. In the Anglo-American adult education literature the work of such writers as Fred Schied (1993), Mike Newman (1993, 1995), Mechthild Hart, (1992), Michael Welton (1987a, 1991), Colin Griffin (1983, 1987), John Field (1991), Frank Adams (1975, 1988), Paul Armstrong (1988), John Wallis and Paula Allman (Allman, 1988; Wallis and Allman, 1996; Allman and Mayo, 1997), Jane Thompson (1980, 1983, 1997; Mayo and Thompson, 1995) and John McIlroy (1995, 1996; McIlroy and Westwood, 1993) has also been informed by historical materialist theory and socialist politics. There is also significant work on independent-working class education, much of it by scholars from outside adult education (Simon, 1965, 1972, 1990; Johnson, 1979, 1988). Then there is the very significant Latin American Marxist literature on education, most widely known through the work of Paulo Freire (1972a; 1972b), but also including the important contributions of Gadotti (1996), Carlos Torres (1990, 1995; Morrow and Torres, 1995), and Timothy Ireland (1987).

Yet overall, in more recent 'radical' Anglo-American adult education theory, the emphasis has been on ideology rather than on political economy, on Habermas and Foucault rather than on Marx and Braverman. The negative effects of this emphasis are best demonstrated through a discussion of examples. Over the past several years there has been a debate in the mainstream adult education literature about the relationship of social movements and adult education. It has been argued, correctly I think, that social movements are important sites of emancipatory adult learning and that more attention needs to be paid to this dimension of their activity. But much of this discussion has been abstract and exhortatory. A lot of energy has gone into debating the distinction between 'old' and 'new' social movements. Social movements have been discussed in general terms – there has been almost no extended analysis of specific social movements or instances of social action. Participants in the discussion have generally written from the perspective of adult education theory or profession, rather than from the perspective of social movement actors or a broader social interest.[2]

Articles by Michael Welton (1993c) and John Holford (1995) are representative. The focus of Welton's paper is new social movements (peace, feminist, ecological, local and personal autonomy) as sites of 'social revolutionary' learning. He sees the goal of these movements as 'defence of the threatened lifeworld and ecosystem' and the creation of 'an autonomous and exuberant civil society'. The demon in Welton's analysis is the State, and to a lesser extent, corporations. He opens his paper with a quote from the social movement theorist Alain Touraine: 'It is our main task now – as it always was – to resuscitate social relations, opposition, defiance, struggle and hope wherever they have been crushed, which is always the order of the state'. Welton himself sees 'the state and corporate steering mechanisms intrud[ing] illegitimately into the lifeworld, threatening human capacity for self-realisation, autonomous learning and active participation in public life as citizens, clients and consumers'. He argues that in western countries in the period 1945–70 welfare capitalism created a 'crisis of the lifeworld'. The social system was run by interest groups and elites. It delivered reasonable social security but discouraged political participation and produced 'egoism, particularism and self-interest'. New social movements have emerged in opposition to these tendencies, committed to rebuilding society on principles of ecological sustainability, social responsibility, grassroots democracy and non-violence. To be put into practice, these principles require a fundamental perceptual transformation, an 'unblocking of communicative learning processes'.

There are a number of problems with Welton's analysis. One is that it is very general. There is no extended analysis of specific social movements or instances of social action. Social movements with disparate goals and interests are named 'new social movements', raising questions about what the term actually means. Particularly puzzling is the inclusion of the bourgeois and radically individualistic interest in personal autonomy as a social movement. Another problem is a flawed analysis of the current crisis of western capitalism, which Welton sees as a crisis of the 'lifeworld', with its origin in the 1960s' recognition that civil society, the third world and the natural environment were regulated, dominated, colonised and brutalised. While these forms of domination do exist and have generated social movement responses, they have all been created by capitalism, a fact that Welton fails to mention. Further, the welfare state has not simply been a means of domination. In the brief 'golden age' of capitalism, the welfare state guaranteed full employment and a living wage and provided social services, including the very university system in which Welton works (Castles, 1985; Esping-Andersen, 1990; Hobsbawm, 1994: 281–4). The real crisis of our time is a crisis of capitalism as it undergoes one of its periodic restructurings in order to become yet more exploitative, productive and profitable. As we saw in Chapter 5, for most people the contemporary problem of the State is not its 'invasion of the lifeworld' but its transformation from a welfare state to a competitive state, facilitating the reorganisation of national and global capitalism. The inadequacy of Welton's analysis springs from his adoption of a variant of European critical theory derived from the Frankfurt School, which privileges ideological domination and de-emphasises both agency and political economy (on these tendencies in the Frankfurt School, see Wood, 1995: 104). Welton's use of critical theory leads him into abstracted analysis and rhetorical turns ('Are the diverse forms of protest crystallising into a historically new social movement? One cannot answer this definitely.' 1993c: 160), the antithesis of the rich and complex pictures of learning and struggle he has painted in his fine historical work (Welton, 1987b, 1991).

The other paper I will examine here also marginalises political economy and agency. Holford (1995) surveys social movement theory and discusses why it has to date had little impact on adult education theory. Drawing on Eyerman and Jamison (1991), Holford suggests that social movements can be usefully seen as 'cognitive praxis'. As social movements develop they create new ways of understanding the world. 'Movement intellectuals' play a crucial role in this, articulating the world view and identity of movements and communicating these to the wider society. Holford maintains that 'it is in the essence of movement intellectuals that they articulate, interpret, lead'. Further,

> The notion of the movement intellectual is the key in an adult education analysis of social movements for it allows us to focus on the role of adult education as an agent of social change. Adult educators who see their role as working with (or even initiating) a movement are seeking to play a part in formulating and structuring its organisational knowledge. This tradition has been central, for example, to the perspectives of much workers' education. (Holford, 1995: 106)

There is a need, Holford argues, for research on the educational role of movement intellectuals.

Holford's argument brings to mind a question posed by Welton (1993c: 135–41) in another paper. What, he asks, is the proper object of adult education as a field of study? What will be researched and theorised? For Holford the interest is in studying the educational role of intellectuals in social movements. Now, while this is an issue worth researching, it is not all there is to education and learning in social movements and it is a different object of study from that of this book – the informal and incidental learning of participants in social movements, social action and community organisations. No doubt we need to research both. But we also need to ask ourselves which is the more important and what are the likely effects of studying one rather than the other. The choice of object of study, and theoretical framework, are political and ethical issues. Holford's focus on intellectuals and adult educators reinforces the identification of adult learning with adult education as a field of professional practice, an identification with which he expresses some discomfort in the same paper (1995: 96–7, 108–9). He also distorts Gramsci's notion of organic intellectual. Gramsci's interest was in intellectuals – specifically proletarian intellectuals – who were an organic part of a class: they were of a class and worked for that class. At one point in his paper Holford turns this notion into a vanguardist conception of an intellectual stratum providing 'direction' to social movements (1995: 107); in another he suggests that adult educators can function as 'movement intellectuals', helping with the creation of 'a communicative culture – organisational knowledge' in social movements (1995: 109).

Holford's paper is also representative of another disturbing tendency in purportedly 'critical' adult education scholarship, its eclectic and rhetorical use of post-modern and post-structuralist theory. In his paper, Holford discusses the question of whether adult education has ever been a social movement. In the course of this discussion he makes these claims:

> The growth of adult education in Europe and North America has been linked to the discourses of modernity, to the great secular movements of industrial capitalism: urbanisation, the emergence of labour, democratisation and modernisation. The adult education movement was a constructed discourse, teleologically imposed on the past by historians who were also major figures in university adult education at the height of its influence in the 1950s and 1960s. ... From a 1990s perspective, nineteenth and early twentieth century adult education appears rather as a spectrum of movements. Yet they did overlap: they shared in particular what Johnson (1988) called a 'rather unreasonable faith in reason'. ... To a postmodern eye, adult education's faith in the possibility of truth may seem naive ... (Holford, 1995: 108–9)

Yet, Holford argues, the notion of adult education as a movement can still make sense if we focus on the relationship of knowledge creation and identity in the formation and evolution of social movements. 'Adult education knowledge – in the specific forms that it has taken – may be contingent upon the creation of an adult education identity, of a self-image of a "movement" as embodying ideals and ethics'.

Let us look closely at Holford's argument and the theory underpinning it. Holford claims, consecutively, that: adult education has been linked (by which people or what social forces, in what ways, with what effects he does not say) to the 'discourses of modernity'; that the adult education movement is a discursive construction of academics; that adult education can still be a social movement in our time if it creates 'an adult education identity' or 'self-image'. Leaving aside the issue of what is actually meant by these claims, they all rest on the post-structuralist assumption that social identities and social movements are discursively constructed. In other words, a social movement, such as the labour movement, or a person's identity as a worker, a woman or an Aboriginal – or all three – are brought into life by ideas and language. Complex historical processes are reduced to changes in language and ideas.[3] The complex interplay of changes in the political economy, organisational politics, ideology and discourse which created modern social movements and contemporary Anglo-American adult education theory are not discussed.

As the historian E. H. Carr pointed out long ago, the analysis you develop is a function of the data you select and the theory you use, and both of these are determined by what you are interested in (cited in Schied, 1995: 235). For too long adult education research and scholarship has focused on the minutae of individual learning and the very restricted area of formal education. Its theorising has frequently been trivial and politically timid. The academic field of adult education has reinforced the neglect of adult education and learning in emancipatory social movements and mainstream social policy. Those of us with an interest in learning as a dimension of use values and emancipatory social action have a very different object of study and need to develop theory which is radically different from, and oppositional to, mainstream adult education theory.

Modern Anglo-American adult education theory has consistently avoided these issues, initially through a narrow instrumentalism which defined adult education in terms of techniques of teaching and curriculum development, then through a humanism that valorised the individual, and most recently through an abstract and professionalised 'critical' theory. Adult education theory, by diverting attention from the social role of adult education, functions, often in subtle – and, sometimes perhaps, unintended – ways, as an ideological support for capitalism. The examples discussed in this section are representative of this process, as is the work on competency-based learning discussed briefly in Chapter 5 (pp. 83–4).

A critique of capitalism[4] must be at the heart of emancipatory adult education theory. Capitalism is the thread that connects the case studies in this book. All the people discussed in this book – American working women, Zimbabwean guerrillas, Australian environmentalists, and Brazilian and Australian women – struggled and learned in capitalist society. In Chapter 5 I pointed out that, because capitalism rests on the private expropriation of surplus labour, it is intrinsically unstable. The continual and accelerating exploitation of labour and nature on which capitalism depends generates economic and ecological crises which can only ever be temporarily resolved. In our time capitalism appears to have reached some sort of watershed. Conservative theorists herald 'the end of history'. The increasing influence of transnational corporations, the collapse of state socialism in eastern Europe, and the rapid industrialisation of Asian and Latin American countries are said to indicate that there is now and will only ever be one way of organising production: capitalism. But socialists see another sort of watershed. While they concede that the whole world is now being penetrated by capitalism, they predict that this process will generate social and environmental chaos. As the Indian Marxist scholar Aijaz Ahmad (1992: 315–16) has pointed out, the development of European and North American capitalism cannot be replicated in the rest of the world – there are insufficient natural resources, and nowhere to send surplus populations. The fatal contradiction in capitalism is that it cannot provide for most of the people whom it has now drawn into its orbit. Negation of this contradiction can only come from a system of production based on fundamentally different premises: production for use, rather than profit; social rather than private expropriation of surplus labour; sustainable production rather than a spiral of growth; cooperation rather than competition among producers. And as Ahmad notes, the name of this negation is socialism.

## Directions

> However difficult it may be to construct socialist practice out of popular consciousness, there is ... no other material out of which it can be constructed and no other socialism that is consistent with both political realism and democratic values. (Wood, 1995: 103)

We live in a contradictory time. Never has socialism been so discredited; never has there been a greater need for it. For without the countervailing force of actually-existing socialism, flawed as it was, and the hope of building something better, we are headed back with frightening speed to the social jungle that Upton Sinclair (1981) described in his novel of working-class life in early twentieth-century Chicago. The great lesson of our century is that socialism cannot

exist without democracy. The question then is, how to build a democratic socialism? I think part of the answer lies in developing an
understanding of learning in popular struggle.

All of the studies in this book are stories of struggle with
authoritarianism. The American women campaigning to reopen the
gynaecological clinic had to combat the arrogance of doctors, hospital
adminstrators and committee members. In the Terania Creek campaign the authority of the foresters, supposedly built on their technical
expertise, was revealed to be power conferred on them by the State
and the industry. The core activists in that campaign also had to
monitor their own tendency towards unilateral decision-making. So
did workers and committee members in the women's neighbourhood
houses. In the Australian mine, workers delighted in subverting the
authoritarianism of managers. In Brazil, working-class women challenged the authoritarianism of the State, the church, the Left, their
husbands and middle-class women. The Zimbabwe liberation struggle,
having overthrown the colonial state, foundered on the authoritarianism of nationalist politicians.

The activists we have met in this book all had a clear idea of what
they wanted: a rainforest for future generations, a clinic where women
would receive affordable and dignified health care, neighbourhood
houses where women could care for their children and develop themselves, workplaces where workers would be treated with respect,
neighbourhoods with decent social services, a country without exploitation or oppression. Some of these goals were more attainable
than others, and all the struggles had their complexities, ambiguities
and contradictions. It is such complexities that educators and activists
struggling to build democratic and socialist relationships must come
to grips with and find a way through.

Much remains to be discovered about the characteristics, determinants, dynamics and effects of learning in popular movements and
struggles. The potential field of study is huge and almost untouched.
Detailed accounts of particular struggles exist in the literatures of
labour history, women's history, urban studies, development studies
and associated fields. The learning dimension can be 'read into' such
studies, in the way I have done in Chapters 2 and 6 of this book, and
much more needs to be done in this regard. In addition, there is an
infinite number of researchable contemporary movements, struggles
and sites. In my experience, activists are generally most willing to

cooperate with researchers who share their broad political goals and who can help them to understand their situations more clearly and act on them more effectively. Two examples will illustrate what might be done.

In the 1970s and 1980s pioneering work was done, much of it by radical feminist scholars, on the intersection of gender and class in US labour history. The methodology of much of this research is similar to that of this book, with detailed accounts of particular struggles being placed within an analysis of broader historical forces. This work is often concerned with the development of women's political consciousness, and the relationship of that consciousness to political action. While these studies do not deal explicitly with learning in struggle, much can be deduced from them. So, for example, accounts of a landmark female garment workers' strike in New York in 1910 give a vivid sense of what and how working women learned as they took direct action (Tax, 1980). Consider this contemporary description of how the strike was initiated by a rank-and-file activist:

> Down the body of the hall arose a working girl, a striker, an unknown, who asked the chairman for the privilege of the floor. Many grumbling dissensions came her way, some excitement was visible on the platform, but the chairman held that as she was a striker she had as good a right there as himself, so Clara Lemlich made her way to the platform. She was a striker from the Leiserson shop; she had been assaulted while picketing; she knew from actual experience what her sisters were up against, and that they were tired of oratory; she knew that they had come there for business; she knew they were seething with discontent and hatred of their bondage; that they were pulsing with sympathy for their fellow workers and that each was ready, aye anxious, for the charge into the camp of the common oppressor, and ... after an impromptu philippic in Yiddish, eloquent even to American ears, she put the motion for a general strike, and was unanimously endorsed. (Tax, 1980: 207)

Clara Lemlich acted in part against monopolisation of this strike meeting by male unionists. Her intervention set off a strike which at its height involved 30,000 workers. Within a few months, however, the strike had been settled in the interests of garment factory owners. This was brought about through a combination of police action, ethnic divisions among the workers, the 'moderating' influence of bourgeois supporters of the strikers, and the machinations of the male union establishment (Tax, 1980: 220–40). And it was not only the strike that was settled in 1910. Two years later a feminist activist noted that female garment workers had 'no place and probably mostly no voice' in their union. More than half a century later there had been little change. In 1970 women comprised 80 per cent of union membership yet had only one seat on the union's executive board (1980: 317). The model of unionism forged early in the century still held, a model which 'put stability in the industry first, followed by good fringe benefits and services to ... members, who were expected to show their desire for a job and their appreciation of their union by remaining in their place' (1980: 240). As Tax notes, this approach to unionism demobilised women workers and made the struggle for women's liberation inseparable from the struggle for economic justice.

Participation in industrial action can be educative for workers. But the story of the 1910 garment workers suggests that the experience of union membership can generate negative, profoundly disempowering, learning. This, of course, is an issue raised by much labour history, in the United States and elsewhere. To take another example. William Serrin's book, *Homestead* (1993), tells the dispiriting story of a Pennsylvania steel town, from its establishment in the 1870s to the closure of its steel mill in 1986. Homestead is known in US labour history for a strike in 1892 which was notable for both its worker solidarity and organisation and for the ferocity with which it was suppressed by corporation and state (Serrin, 1993: 66–95). The defeat of the strike and the measures subsequently taken by the corporation – which included incentives like provision of housing, sports facilities, libraries and worker shareholdings, as well as coercive measures including 'spies, blacklisting, suppression of wages, payoffs for jobs and advancement, corruption of priests and ministers, gifts to communities, control of borough governments, exploitation of ethnic and racial differences, and countenancing corruption' (1993: 165) – de-unionised the town for forty years. And when the union returned, it came in the form of the United Steel Workers of America, which struck deals with the corporation that enriched the union leadership, brought benefits to workers during the boom time for steel during and after World War Two, but did nothing to protect workers' long-term interests, thus helping to pave the way to the mill closure.

As with the garment workers' strike, Homestead's history suggests that in struggle workers can learn defeatism, withdrawal and passivity, and that workers' failure to control their own organisations is both a determinant and an outcome of this negative learning. These two examples also raise the question of what the working class as a whole has learned from its experience over the past century. In recent years, all over the western world workers have allowed jobs and working conditions, gained through generations of struggle, to be taken away from them. This is not to blame but to seek to explain, and to leaven any feelings of unrealistic optimism which might be created through reading the case studies in this book. In 1961 Raymond Williams articulated the notion of the 'long revolution', the progressive expansion of economic, political and educational participation in the modern era, won through popular struggle. Today, in an era in which capital has so effectively regained the initiative, this notion of cumulative, if hard won, gains is harder to support. But if working-class gains have been so readily reversed, we need to ask why. And in exploring this question we need to revisit popular movements and struggles. As we do this we will find signposts to where we need to go. Sometimes the findings will be fairly gloomy, as in the two US examples just discussed. Other situations will yield more optimistic insights, as do the case studies in Chapters 2–6 of this book. But, to reiterate a point made in relation to these studies, we need to recognise the complex, ambiguous and contradictory character of particular movements and struggles. Analyses of these complexities provide a necessary basis for future strategies.

I have argued in this book that popular struggles and movements have a, so far little studied, learning dimension, which when examined yields insights into the dynamics and effects of social movement activity. In discussing this learning dimension I have paid particular attention to the warp and weft of reproduction and recognition in people's consciousness in particular struggles and sites. I am convinced that an understanding of these learning processes in past and present struggles is crucial to the development of a truly emancipatory education and politics in our time. I hope that this book throws light on the nature of these learning processes, and suggests directions for further research and action.

## Notes

1. I always feel uneasy when I speak as if there is 'a' body of adult education theory. The body of work to which I refer is, of course, that work

to which many readers of this book have been exposed, and that is largely US and English material. The cultural exclusions of this body of material are beginning to be discussed (see, for example, Cunningham, 1991), and much more could be said about them. Here, however, I simply want to note the problematic nature of the notion of 'adult education theory'.

2. This debate has been conducted in the US journal *Adult Education Quarterly*. In addition to the articles by Welton and Holford discussed here, see Finger, 1989 and Spencer, 1995. As far as I am aware, the only case studies of learning in social action or social movements are those collected and edited by Mike Welton in the special issue of *Convergence* on 'liberatory movements' (Vol. XXVI, No. 4, 1993b), Welton's (1987b, 1991) studies of working-class learning in Canada, and my own work.

3. Holford might not have intended this, but this is the effect of his analysis. This is what post-structuralism is, a form of analysis that valorises one variable, discourse, and is thereby, in the strict sense, both idealist and simplistic. For critiques of post-structuralism, see Ahmad, 1992: especially 3–6, 35–6, 68–70; and Wood, 1986: 61–78, the latter built around a critique of Laclau and Mouffe, 1985.

4. A reader of the manuscript of this book asked, 'How about the critique of patriarchy? Or racism for that matter?' I agree that a critique of both need also to be central to emancipatory education theory. But in the discussion here I wish to confront the dearth of analysis of capitalism and class in contemporary 'radical' adult education theory, which reflects the tendencies in contemporary social science referred to on pp. 137–8, and which diverts activists from truly radical – that is, democratic and socialist – politics and economics.

# Bibliography

## Archives

National Archives of Zimbabwe (NAZ) material in Harare includes colonial correspondence files (S1542 and other serial numbers) and newspapers: *Bantu Mirror, The African Weekly, Rhodesian Weekly Review. The Rhodesian Herald* is held in the library of *The Zimbabwe Herald* in Harare.

## Newspapers

*National Times (NT); Nimbin News; The Northern Start (NS); The Daily News (DN); The Australian.*

## Books and other print materials

ACTU/TDC (1987). *Australia Reconstructed*, Canberra: Australian Government Publishing Service

Adams, Frank (1975). *Unearthing Seeds of Fire. The Idea of Highlander*, Winston-Salem: John Blair

Adams, F. (1988). Worker ownership: an opportunity to control the production of knowledge. In T. Lovett (ed.), *Radical Approaches to Adult Education: A Reader*, London: Routledge

Ahmad, A. (1992). *In Theory: Classes, Nations, Literatures*, London: Verso

Alinsky, S. (1971). *Rules for Radicals. A Pragmatic Reader for Realistic Radicals*, New York: Random House

Allman, P. (1988). Gramsci, Freire and Illich: their contributions to education for socialism. In T. Lovett (ed.), *Radical Approaches to Adult Education: A Reader*, London: Routledge

Allman, P. and Mayo, P. (1997). Freire, Gramsci and globalisation: some implications for social and political commitment in adult education. In *Proceedings of 1997 International SCUTREA/AERC/AAACE Conference*, London: Birkbeck College, University of London

Alvarez, S. (1989). Politicizing gender and engendering democracy. In A. Stephen (ed.), *Democratizing Brazil: Problems of Transition and Consolidation*, New York: Oxford University Press

— (1990a). Women's participation in the Brazilian 'People's Church': a critical appraisal, *Feminist Studies*, Vol. 16, No. 2, pp. 381–409

— (1990b). *Engendering Democracy in Brazil: Women's Movements in Transition Politics*, Princeton, NJ: Princeton University Press

Alves, M. H. M. (1984). Grassroots organisations, trade unions, and the church: a challenge to the controlled *Abertura* in Brazil, *Latin American Perspectives*, Vol. 11, No. 1, pp. 73–102

— (1985). *State and Opposition in Military Brazil*, Austin: University of Texas Press

Andrewson, A. M. (1949). Who are Gentlemen?, *Bantu Mirror*, 17/12/1949, p. 9

Anyon, J. (1983). Intersections of gender and class: accommodation and resistance by working class and affluent females to contradictory sex-role ideologies. In S. Walker and L. Barton (eds), *Gender, Class and Education*, New York: Falmer

Armstrong, P. (1988). The long search for the working class: socialism and the education of adults, 1850–1930. In T. Lovett (ed.), *Radical Approaches to Adult Education: A Reader*, London: Routledge

Austin-Broos, D. (1987). Clifford Geertz: culture, sociology and historicism. In D. Austin-Broos (ed.), *Creating Culture: Profiles in the Study of Culture*, Sydney: Allen and Unwin

Ball, S. (ed.) (1990). *Foucault and Education*, London: Routledge

Benson, G. and Saleeba, J. (1984). *Community Learning: A Public Investment* Melbourne: Council of Adult Education

Boud, D. and Walker, D. (1991). *Experience and Learning: Reflection at Work*, Geelong: Deakin University Press

Boud, D., Keogh, R. and Walker, D. (1985). *Reflection: Turning Experience into Learning*, London: Kogan Page

Braverman, H. (1974). *Labour and Monopoly Capital*, New York: Monthly Review Press

Bright, B. (1989). *Theory and Practice in the Study of Adult Education*, London: Routledge

Brookfield, S. (1983). *Adult Learners, Adult Education and the Community*, Milton Keynes: Open University Press

— (1986). *Understanding and Facilitating Adult Learning*, San Francisco: Jossey-Bass

Brown, T. (1997). The economic environment of national training reform. In B. Boughton, T. Brown and G. Foley, *New Directions for Australian Adult Education*, Sydney: Centre for Popular Education, University of Technology, Sydney

— (1999, forthcoming). Challenging globalisation as discourse and phenomenon, *International Journal of Lifelong Education*, Vol. 18, No. 1

Cabral, A. (1973). *Return to the Source: Selected Speeches of Amilcar Cabral*, New York: Monthly Review Press

— (1974). *Revolution in Guinea: An African People's Struggle*, London: Stage 1

Caldeira, T. P. R. (1986–87). Electoral struggles in a neighbourhood in the periphery of São Paulo, *Politics and Society*, Vol. 15, No. 1, pp. 43–66

Cammack, P. (1986). Resurgent democracy: threat and promise, *New Left Review*, No. 157, pp. 121–8

Candy, Philip (1991). *Self-Direction for Lifelong Learning*, San Francisco: Jossey-Bass

Capiora Women's Group (1993). *Women in Brazil*, London: Latin America Bureau

Carr, W. and Kemmis, S. (1986). *Becoming Critical: Education, Knowledge and Action Research*, Geelong: Deakin University Press

Castles, F. (1985). *The Working Class and Welfare*, Sydney: Allen and Unwin

Cerny, P. (1990). *The Changing Architecture of Politics: Structure, Agency and the Future of the State*, London: Sage

Chomsky, N. (1992). *Deterring Democracy*, London: Vintage

— (1993). *Year 501: The Conquest Continues*, London: Verso

Clark, Joy (1986). Community education and the concept of need, *International Journal of Lifelong Education*, Vol. 5, No. 3, pp. 197–205

Clark, M. and Wilson, A. (1991). Context and rationality in Mezirow's theory of transformational learning, *Adult Education Quarterly*, Vol. 41, pp. 75–91

Clarke, S. (1987). *Sharing the House*, Melbourne: Preston College of TAFE

Cliffe, L., Mpofu, J. and Munslow, B. (1980). Nationalist politics in Zimbabwe: the 1980 elections and beyond, *Review of African Political Economy*, No. 18, pp. 44–67

Collard, S. and Law, M. (1989). The limits of perspective transformation: a critique of Mezirow's theory, *Adult Education Quarterly*, Vol. 39, pp. 99–107

Collins, M. (1991). *Adult Education as Vocation: A Critical Role for the Adult Educator in Today's Society*, London: Routledge

Costello, C. (1988). Women workers and collective action: a case study from the insurance industry. In A. Brookman and S. Morgen (eds), *Women and the Politics of Empowerment*, Phildelphia: Temple University Press

(CPAE) Commission of Professors of Adult Education (1991). *Proceedings of the 1991 Annual Conference*, Harrisburg: Pennsylvania State University

Cunningham, P. (1991). International influences in the development of knowledge. In J. Peters, P. Jarvis and Associates, *Adult Education: Evolution and Achievements of a Developing Field of Study*, San Francisco: Jossey-Bass, pp. 347–83

Curtain, R. et al. (1991). *Award Restructuring and Workplace Reform: An Appraisal of Progress based upon 33 Case Studies*, Melbourne: National Key Centre for Industrial Relations

Curthoys, A. (1988). Concepts in social theory. In G. Kress (ed.), *Communica-*

*tion and Culture: An Introduction*, Sydney: New South Wales University Press

Danaher, K. and Shellenberger, M. (eds) (1995). *Fighting for the Soul of Brazil*, New York: Monthly Review Press

Devos, A. (1991). Flexibility rules, OK? MEd Seminar Paper: School of Adult and Language Education, University of Technology, Sydney

Dunk, T., McBride, S. and Nelsen, R. (1996). *The Training Trap: Ideology, Training and the Labour Market*. Special issue of *Socialist Studies*, Vol. 11. Winnipeg/Halifax: Society for Socialist Studies/Fernwood Publishing

Eagleton, T. (1989). *Raymond Williams: Critical Perspectives*, Cambridge: Polity Press

Ellsworth, E. (1989). Why doesn't this feel empowering? Working through the repressive myths of critical pedagogy, *Harvard Educational Review*, Vol. 59, No. 3, pp. 297–324

Emery, F. (1991a). From Bear Mountain to workplace Australia. In *Designing the Future: Workplace Reform in Australia*. Conference Papers, Melbourne: Workplace Australia, pp. 103–18

— (1991b). The light on the hill. In *Designing the Future: Workplace Reform in Australia*. Conference Papers, Melbourne: Workplace Australia, pp. 191–201

Esping-Andersen, G. (1990). *The Tree Worlds of Welfare Capitalism*, Cambridge: Polity Press

Ewer, P., Hampson, I., Lloyd, C., Rainford, J., Rix, S. and Smith, M. (eds) (1991). *Politics and the Accord*, Sydney: Pluto Press

Eyerman, R. and Jamison, A. (1991). *Social Movements: A Cognitive Approach*, Cambridge: Polity Press

Fairclough, N. (1992). *Discourse and Social Change*, Cambridge: Polity Press

Field, J. (1991). Competency and the pedagogy of labour, *Studies in the Education of Adults*, Vol. 23, pp. 41–52

Field, L. (1995). *Managing Organisational Learning: From Rhetoric to Reality*, Melbourne: Longman

Finger, M. (1989). New social movements and their implications for adult education, *Adult Education Quarterly*, Vol. 40, No. 1, pp. 15–22

Flora, C. B. (1984). Socialist feminism in Latin America, *Women and Politics*, Vol. 4, No. 1, pp. 69–93

Foley, G. (1978). Some international aspects of the Zimbabwe 'settlement', *World Review*, Vol. 17, No. 2, pp. 17–26

— (1981). Learning in the struggle: the development of political consciousness among Zimbabweans in the 1930s, *Zimbabwe History*, Vol. XII, pp. 47–65

— (1982). Political economy and education in Zimbabwe, 1980–1982. Henderson Seminar Paper No. 52, Harare: Department of History, University of Zimbabwe, August

— (1984a). Education and social change in Zimbabwe, 1890–1962. PhD thesis, University of Sydney

— (1984b). Education and politics within the Zimbabwe liberation struggle, 1961–1979. Part 2: Struggles within the struggle. Unpublished paper, Sydney College of Advanced Education, April

— (1991a). *Terania Creek: Learning in a Green Campaign*, Sydney: School of Adult Education, University of Technology, Sydney, typescript 45 pp.

— (1991b). Terania Creek: learning in a green campaign, *Australian Journal of Adult and Community Education*, Vol. 31, No. 3, pp. 160–76

— (1991c). Radical adult education. In M. Tennant (ed.), *Australian Adult Education: Issues and Practices*, London: Routledge

— (1992). Adult education and the labour market. In R. Harris and P. Willis (eds), *Striking a Balance: Adult and Community Education in Australia towards 2000*, Adelaide: University of South Australia, pp. 46–65

— (1993a). The neighbourhood house: site of struggle, site of learning, *British Journal of Sociology of Education*, Vol. 14, pp. 21–37

— (1993b). Struggling over the cost of schooling: the 1964 schools boycott in Zimbabwe and its aftermath, *History of Education Review*, Vol. 22, pp. 1–15

— (1993c). Political education in the Chinese liberation struggle, *International Journal of Lifelong Education*, Vol. 13, No. 1, pp. 323–42

— (1993d). Progressive but not socialist: political education in the Zimbabwe liberation struggle, *Convergence*, Vol. XXVII, No. 4, pp. 79–88

— (1994). Adult education and capitalist reorganisation, *Studies in the Education of Adults*, Vol. 26, No. 2, pp. 121–43

— (1995a). Domination and resistance in workers' political learning. Paper presented at annual conference of the Canadian Association of Adult Education, Montreal: Concordia University, June

— (1995b). *Understanding Adult Education and Training*, Sydney: Allen and Unwin

Foley, G. and Flowers, R. (1992). Knowledge and power in Aboriginal adult education, *Convergence*, Vol. XXV, No. 1, pp. 61–74

Franzway, S., Court, D. and Connell, R. W. (1989). *Staking a Claim: Feminism, Bureaucracy and the State*, Sydney: Allen and Unwin

Freedman, R. (ed.) (1961). *Marx on Economics*, Harmondsworth: Penguin

Freire, Paulo (1972a). *Cultural Action for Freedom*, Harmondsworth: Penguin

— (1972b). *Pedagogy of the Oppressed*, Harmondsworth: Penguin

Gadotti, M. (1996). *Pedagogy of Practice: A dialectical philosophy of education*, Albany: SUNY Press

Galeano, E. (1973). *Open Veins of Latin America: Five Centuries of the Pillage of a Continent*, New York: Monthly Review Press

— (1989). *Century of the Wind*, Harmondsworth: Penguin

— (1992). *We Say No: Chronicles 1963–1991*, New York: Norton

Game, A. (1991). *Undoing the Social: Towards a Deconstructive Sociology*, Toronto: University of Toronto Press

Geertz, C. (1973). Thick description: toward an interpretive theory of culture. In C. Geertz, *The Interpretation of Cultures. Selected Essays*, London: Fontana

— (1988). *Works and Lives: The Anthropologist as Author*, Stanford, CA: Stanford University Press

Gelpi, E. (1979). *A Future for Lifelong Education*, Manchester: Department of Adult and Higher Education, University of Manchester

— (1985). *Lifelong Education and International Relations*, Vols 1 and 2, London: Croom Helm

Genovese, E. (1974). *Roll, Jordan, Roll: The World the Slaves Made*, New York: Pantheon Books

Giroux, H. (1984). Ideology, agency and the process of schooling. In S. Walker and L. Barton (eds), *Social Crisis and Education Research*, London: Croom Helm

Gonczi, A. (ed.) (1992). *Developing a Competent Workforce: Adult Learning Strategies for Vocational Educators and Trainers*, Adelaide: National Centre for Vocational Education and Research

Gowen, S. (1991). Beliefs about literacy: measuring women into silence/hearing women into speech, *Discourse and Society*, Vol. 2, No. 4, pp. 439–50

Gramsci, A. (1971). *Selections from the Prison Notebooks*, New York: International Publishers

Gravell, A. and Nelson, C. (1986). *The Association of Neighbourhood Houses 150th Project*, Melbourne: Association of Neighbourhood Learning Centres

Griffin, Colin (1983). *Curriculum Theory in Adult and Lifelong Education*, London: Croom Helm

— (1987). *Adult Education and Social Policy*, London: Croom Helm

Hager, P. and Gonczi, A. (1991). Competency-based standards: a boon for continuing professional education?, *Studies in Continuing Education,* Vol. 13, pp. 24–40

Hall, B. (1993). Re-centering adult education research: whose world is first?, *Studies in Continuing Education*, Vol. 15, No. 2, 1993, pp. 149–61

Hampson, I. (1991). Post-Fordism, the 'French Regulation School', and the work of John Mathews, *Journal of Australian Political Economy*, Vol. 28, pp. 92–130

Hart, M. (1990a). Liberation through consciousness-raising. In J. Mezirow (ed.), *Fostering Critical Reflection in Adulthood*, San Francisco: Jossey-Bass

— (1990b). Critical theory and beyond: further perspectives on emancipatory learning, *Adult Education Quarterly*, Vol. 40, No. 3, pp. 125–38

— (1992). *Working and Education for Life*, London: Routledge

Harvey, D. (1989). *The Condition of Post-Modernity*, Oxford: Basil Blackwell

Head, D. (1977). Education at the bottom, *Studies in Adult Education*, Vol. 9, No. 2, pp. 127–52

Herman, E. S. and Petras, J. (1985). Resurgent democracy: rhetoric and reality, *New Left Review*, No. 154, pp. 83–98

Hobsbawm, E. (1994). *The Age of Extremes: The Short Twentieth Century*, London: Michael Joseph

Holford, J. (1995). Why social movements matter: adult education theory, cognitive praxis and the creation of knowledge, *Adult Education Quarterly*, Vol. 45, No. 2, pp. 95–111

Horne, D. (ed.) (1992). *The Trouble with Economic Rationalism*, Melbourne: Scribe

Horton, M., with Kohl, J. and H. (1990). *The Long Haul: An Autobiography*, New York: Doubleday

Hyman, R. (1991). *Plus ça change?* The theory of production and the production of theory. In A. Pollert (ed.), *Farewell to Flexibility?*, Oxford: Basil Blackwell

Ireland, T. (1979). *Gelpi's View of Lifelong Education*, Manchester: Department of Adult and Higher Education, University of Manchester

— (1987). *Antonio Gramsci and Adult Education: Reflections on the Brazilian Experience*, Manchester: Department of Adult and Higher Education, University of Manchester

Johnson, R. (1979). Really useful knowledge: radical education and working class culture, 1790–1848. In J. Clarke, C. Critcher and R. Johnson (eds), *Working Class Culture: Studies in History and Theory*, London: Hutchinson

— (1988). Really useful knowledge, 1790–1850: memories for education in the 1980s. In T. Lovett (ed.), *Radical Approaches to Adult Education: A Reader*, London: Routledge

Johnson, R. and Hinton, F. (1986). *It's Human Nature: Adult and Continuing Education in Australia*, Canberra: Commonwealth Tertiary Education Commission

Keck, M. E. (1986–87). Democratization and dissension: the formation of the Worker's Party, *Politics and Society*, Vol. 15, No. 1, pp. 67–95

Kemmis, S. and Fitzclarence, L. (1986). *Curriculum Theorising: Beyond Reproduction Theory*, Geelong: Deakin University Press

Kimberley, H. (1986). *Community Learning: The Outcomes Report*, Melbourne: Victorian TAFE Board

Kinloch, G. C. (1974). Changing black reaction to white domination, *Rhodesian History*, Vol. 5, pp. 67–78

Knight, J., Lingard, B. and Porter, P. (eds) (1991). Introduction. In B. Lingard, J. Knight and P. Porter (eds), *Schooling Reform in Hard Times*, New York: Falmer

Kowarick, L. (1985). The pathways to encounter: reflections on the social struggle in São Paulo. In D. Slater (ed.), *New Social Movements and the State in Latin America*, Amsterdam: CEDLA

Laclau, E. and Mouffe, C. (1985). *Hegemony and Socialist Strategy: Towards a Radical Democratic Politics*, London: Verso

Lather, P. (1986). Issues of validity in openly ideological research: between a rock and a hard place, *Interchange*, Vol. 17, No. 4, pp. 63–84

Latin America Bureau (1982). *Brazil State and Struggle*, London: Latin America Bureau

Lears, T. J. (1985). The concept of cultural hegemony, *The American Historical Review*, Vol. 90, pp. 567–93

Leymann, H. and Kornbluth, H. (1989). *Socialisation and Learning at Work*, London: Gower

Linden, I. (1980). *The Catholic Church and the Struggle for Zimbabwe*, London: Longman

Lingard, B. (1991). Corporate federalism: the emerging approach to policy-making for Australian schools. In B. Lingard, J. Knight and P. Porter (eds), *Schooling Reform in Hard Times*, New York: Falmer

Lovett, T. (1975). *Adult Education, Community Development and the Working Class*, London: Ward Lock

— (1985). *Radical Approaches to Adult Education: A Reader*, London: Routledge

Lovett, T., Clarke, C. and Kilmurray, A. (1983). *Adult Education and Community Action*, London: Croom Helm

Luttrell, W. (1988). The Edison school struggle: the reshaping of working-class education and women's consciousness. In A. Brookman and S. Morgen (eds), *Women and the Politics of Empowerment*, Philadelphia: Temple University Press

McAdam, D. (1982). *Political Process and the Development of Black Insurgency, 1930–1970*, Chicago: Chicago University Press

McIlroy, J. (1995). The dying of the light? A radical look at trade union education. In M. Mayo and J. Thompson (eds), *Adult Learning, Critical Intelligence and Social Change*, Leicester: National Institute of Adult Continuing Education

— (1996). *From the Great Tradition to NVQs: universities and trade unions in the fin de siecle*. In J. Wallis (ed.), *Liberal Adult Education: The End of an Era?*, Nottingham: Continuing Education Press/University of Nottingham

McIlroy, J. and Westwood, S. (1993). *Border Country: Raymond Williams in Adult Education*, Leicester: National Institute of Adult Continuing Education

McIntyre, J. (1996). On becoming a meditator: reflections on adult learning and social context. In P. Willis and B. Neville (eds), *Qualitative Research Practice in Adult Education*, Melbourne: David Lovell Publishing

Mainwaring, S. (1989). Grassroots popular movements and the struggle for democracy: Nova Iguaçu. In A. Stepan (ed.), *Democratizing Brazil: Problems of Transition and Consolidation*, New York: Oxford University Press

Mainwaring, S. and Viola, E. (1984). New social movements, political culture and democracy: Brazil and Argentina in the 1980s, *Telos*, No. 61, pp. 17–52

Marsick, V. (ed.) (1987). *Learning in the Workplace*, London: Croom Helm

Marsick, V. and Watkins, K. (1991). *Informal and Incidental Learning in the Workplace*, London: Routledge

Martin, D. and Johnson, P. (1981). *The Struggle for Zimbabwe*, Harare: Zimbabwe Publishing Company

Mathews, J. (1989a). *Tools of Change*, Melbourne: Pluto Press

— (1989b). *Age of Democracy: The Politics of Post-Fordism*, Melbourne: Oxford University Press

Mayo, M. and Thompson, J. (1995). *Adult Learning, Critical Intelligence and Social Change*, Leicester: National Institute of Adult Continuing Education

Mayo, P. (1993), When does it work? Freire's pedagogy in context, *Studies in the Education of Adults*, Vol. 25, No. 1, pp. 11–27

— (1994). Synthesising Gramsci and Freire: possibilities for a theory of radical adult education, *International Journal of Lifelong Education*, Vol. 13, No. 2, pp. 31–9

— (1995). Critical literacy and emancipatory politics: the work of Paulo Freire, *International Journal of Educational Development*, Vol. 15, No. 4, pp. 363–79

— (1996). Transformative adult education in an age of globalisation: a Gramscian–Freirean synthesis and beyond, *Alberta Journal of Educational Research*, Vol. 42, No. 2, pp. 148–60

— (1997). Tribute to Paulo Freire (1929–1997), *International Journal of Lifelong Education*, Vol. 16, No. 5, pp. 365–70

— (1999). *Gramsci, Freire and Adult Education*, London: Zed

Meredith, M. (1979). *The Past is Another Country*, London: Deutsch.

Metcalfe, A. (1988). *For Freedom and Dignity: Historical Agency and Class Structures in the Coalfields of NSW*, Sydney: Allen & Unwin

Metcalfe, Bill (1986). 'Dropping out and staying in': recruitment, socialisation, engenderment and commitment within contemporary alternative lifestyles. PhD thesis, School of Australian Environmental Studies, Griffith University, Brisbane

Mezirow, Jack (1981). A critical theory of adult learning and education, *Adult Education* (US), Vol. 32, No. 1, pp. 3–27.

— (1991a). *Fostering Critical Reflection in Adulthood*, San Francisco: Jossey-Bass

— (1991b). *Transformative Dimensions of Adult Learning*, San Francisco: Jossey-Bass

Milkman, R. (ed.) (1985). *Women, Work and Protest: A Century of US Women's Labor History*, Boston: Routledge and Kegan Paul

Milner, A. (1991). *Contemporary Cultural Theory: An Introduction*, Sydney: Allen & Unwin

Morgen, S. (1988). 'It's the whole power of the city against us!': the development of political consciousness in a women's health care coalition. In A. Brookman and S. Morgen (eds), *Women and the Politics of Empowerment*, Philadelphia: Temple University Press

Moore, D. (1991). The ideological formation of the Zimbabwean ruling class, *Journal of Southern African Studies*, Vol. 7, No. 3, pp. 472–95

Morrow, R. and Torres, C. A. (1995). *Social Theory and Education: A Critique of Theories of Social and Cultural Reproduction*, Albany: State University of New York Press

Moyers, B. (1981). *Adventures of a Radical Hillbilly* (Video), New York: WNET

Mtmkulu, T. F. (1949). Need for a National Movement, *Bantu Mirror*, 14/5/1949, p. 9

Mubako, S. V. (1976). Aspects of the Zimbabwe liberation movement 1966–1976: part I, *Mohlomi, Journal of Southern African Historical Studies*, Vol. 2, pp. 44–58

Mulligan, M. (1994). Environment and development in Latin America: towards a neostructuralist conception of ecopolitics. PhD thesis, Royal Melbourne Institute of Technology, Melbourne

Neruda, P. (1978). *Memoirs*, Harmondsworth: Penguin

Newman, M. (1993). *The Third Contract: Theory and Practice in Trade Union Training*, Sydney: Stewart Victor Publishing

— (1995). *Defining the Enemy: Adult Education in Social Action*, Sydney: Stewart Victor Publishing

Nicholson, Nan (1982). *Terania Creek*. Typescript: 61 pp.

Nyagumbo, M. (1980). *With the People*, Harare: Graham Publishing

Packenham, R. A. (1986). The changing political discourse in Brazil, 1964–1985. In W. Selcher (ed.), *Political Liberalization in Brazil: Dynamics, Dilemmas, and Future Prospects*, Boulder, CO: Westview Press

Patton, P. (1987). Michel Foucault. In D. Austin-Broos (ed.), *Creating Culture: Profiles in the Study of Culture*, Sydney: Allen and Unwin

Peters, J., Jarvis, P. and associates (1991). *Adult Education: Evolution and Achievements in a Developing Field of Study*, San Francisco: Jossey-Bass

Philp, M. (1985). Michel Foucault. In Q. Skinner (ed.), *The Return of Grand Theory in the Human Sciences*, Cambridge: Cambridge University Press

Pierce, G. (1987). Management workshop: towards a new paradigm. In V. Marsick (ed.), *Learning in the Workplace*, London: Croom Helm

Pilger, J. (1992). *Distant Voices*, London: Vintage

Pollert, A. (ed.) (1991). *Farewell to Flexibility?*, Oxford: Basil Blackwell

Prineas, Peter and Elenius, Elizabeth (n.d.). *Why Log Terania Creek?*, Sydney: NSW National Parks Association

Puelo, M. (1994). *The Struggle is One: Voices and Visions of Liberation*, Albany: State University of New York Press

Pusey, M. (1991). *Economic Rationalism in Canberra*, Cambridge: Cambridge University Press

Ranger, T. (1985). *Peasant Consciousness and Guerrilla War in Zimbabwe*, London:

Rees, S., Rodley, G. and Stilwell, F. (1993). *Beyond the Market: Alternatives to Economic Rationalism*, Sydney: Pluto Press

Rodney, W. (1972). *How Europe Underdeveloped Africa*, London: Bogle-L'Ouverture Publications

Ross, P. and Levy, J. (1989). Written in blood: the Sandinismo Movement of Nicaragua. In C. Jennett and R. Stewart (eds), *Politics of the Future: The Role of Social Movements*, Melbourne: Methuen

Rossing, B. (1991). Patterns of informal learning: insights from community work, *International Journal of Lifelong Education*, Vol. 10, No. 1, pp. 45–60

Rowbotham, S. (1972). *Women, Resistance and Revolution*, Harmondsworth: Penguin

— (1992). *Women in Movement: Feminism and Social Action*, London: Routledge

Saffioti, H. (1978). *Women in Class Society*, New York: Monthly Review Press

Sarti, C. (1989). The panorama of feminism in Brazil, *New Left Review*, No. 173, pp. 75–90

Savage, J. (1991). *Skills Formation through Community-based Providers of Adult and Community Education*. Draft report, Canberra: Australian Association of Adult and Community Education

Schacht, R. (1971). *Alienation*, London: Allen & Unwin

Schied, F. (1993). *Learning in Social Context: Workers and Adult Education in Nineteenth Century Chicago*, DeKalb, IL.: LEPS Press

— (1995) Review of J. Kett (1994). The pursuit of knowledge under difficulties, *Adult Education Quarterly*, Vol. 45, No. 4, pp. 232–35

Schmink, M. (1981). Women in Brazilian *Abertura* politics, *Signs*, Vol. 7, No. 11, pp. 115–34

Schneider, R. M. (1986). Brazil's political future. In W. Selcher (ed.), *Political Liberalization in Brazil: Dynamics, Dilemmas, and Future Prospects*, Boulder, CO: Westview Press

Sebetso, L. M. (1938). What will be the future of native education in this country?, *Bantu Mirror*, Vol. 5, No. 2, pp. 1–10

Selden, M. (1973). People's war and the transformation of peasant societies: China and Vietnam. In L. Kaplan (ed.), *Revolutions: A Comparative Study*, New York: Vintage

Senge, P. (1992). *The Fifth Discipline: The Art and Practice of the Learning Organisation*, London: Century

Serrin, W. (1993). *Homestead: The Glory and Tragedy of an American Steel Town*, New York: Vintage

Shilling, C. (1992). Reconceptualising structure and agency in the sociology of education: structuration theory and schooling, *British Journal of Sociology of Education*, Vol. 13, pp. 69–87

Simon, B. (1965). *Education and the Labour Movement, 1870–1920*, London: Lawrence and Wishart

— (ed.) (1972). *The Radical tradition in education in Britain*, London: Lawrence and Wishart

— (ed.) (1990). *The Search for Enlightenment: The Working Class and Adult Education in the Twentieth Century*, London: Lawrence and Wishart

Sinclair, U. (1981). *The Jungle*, New York: Bantam

Sithole, M. (n.d.). *Zimbabwe: Struggles Within the Struggle*, Harare: Rujeko Publishing

Skeggs, B. (1991). Challenging masculinity and using sexuality, *British Journal of Sociology of Education*, Vol. 12, pp. 127–39

Skinner, Q. (1985). Introduction. In Q. Skinner (ed.), *The Return of Grand Theory in the Social Sciences*, Cambridge: Cambridge University Press

Slater, D. (1985). Social movements and a recasting of the political. In D. Slater (ed.), *New Social Movements and the State in Latin America*, Amsterdam: CEDLA

Smith, D., Simpson, C. and Davies, I. (1981). *Mugabe,* Salisbury: Pioneer Head Press

Spencer, B. (1995). Old and new social movements as learning sites: greening labor unions and unionizing the greens, *Adult Education Quarterly*, Vol. 46, No. 1, pp. 31–42

Stanley, L. (ed.) (1990). *Feminist Praxis*, London: Routledge

Tax, M. (1980). *The Rising of the Women: Feminist Solidarity and Class Conflict, 1880–1917*, New York: Monthly Review Press

Taylor, M. and Bedard, R. (1992). *Proceedings of the Eleventh Annual Conference of CASAE*, Saskatoon: University of Saskatchewan

Tennant, M. (ed.) (1991). *Adult and Continuing Education in Australia,* London: Routledge

Terania Native Forest Action Group (TNFAG) (n.d.) *Facts About the Forests.* Pamphlet: no publishing details.

Thomson, A. (1993). Learning about adult education: the 1992 North American adult education research conferences, *Studies in the Education of Adults*, Vol. 25, pp. 92–104

Thompson, E. P. (1968). *The Making of the English Working Class*, Harmondsworth: Penguin.

Thompson, J. (ed.) (1980). *Adult Education for a Change*, London: Hutchinson

— (1983). *Learning Liberation*, London: Croom-Helm

— (1997). *Words in Edgeways: Radical Learning for Social Change*, Leicester: National Institute of Adult Continuing Education

Torres, C. A. (1990). *The Politics of Non-formal Education in Latin America*, New York: Praeger

Torres, C. A. (ed.) (1995). *Education and Social Change in Latin America*, Albert Park (Vic): James Nicholas

Usher, R. and Bryant, I. (1989). *Adult Education as Theory, Practice and Research*, London: Routledge

Vink, N. (1985). Base communities and urban social movements: a case study of the metalworkers' strike 1980, São Bernardo, Brazil. In D. Slater (ed.), *New Social Movements and the State in Latin America*, Amsterdam: CEDLA

Viola, E. J. (1988). The ecologist movement in Brazil (1974–1986): from environmentalism to ecopolitics, *International Journal of Urban and Regional Research*, Vol. 12, No. 2, pp. 211–28

Walker, Ian (1987). *Bringing Back the Big Scrub Rainforest*, Byron Bay: Jinny Hebb Press

Walker, S. and Barton, L. (eds) (1983). *Gender, Class and Education*, New York: Falmer

— (1984). *Social Crisis and Educational Research*, London: Croom Helm

Wallis, J. and Allman, P. (1996). Adult education, the 'critical' citizen and social change. In J. Wallis (ed.), *Liberal Adult Education: The End of an Era?*, Nottingham: Continuing Education Press, University of Nottingham

Wangoola, P. and Youngman, F. (1996). *Towards a Transformative Political Economy of Adult Education: Theoretical and Practical Challenges*, De Kalb, IL: LEPS Press

Ward, R. (1958). *The Australian Legend*, Melbourne: Oxford University Press

Watson, Ian (1990). *Fighting over the Forests*, Sydney: Allen & Unwin.

Webb, S. (1990). Counter-arguments: an ethnographic look at 'Women and Class'. In L. Stanley (ed.), *Feminist Praxis: Research, Theory and Epistemology in Feminist Sociology*, London: Routledge

Welton, M. (1987a). Vivisecting the nightingale: reflections on adult education as an object of study, *Studies in the Education of Adults*, Vol. 19, pp. 46–68

— (1987b). *Knowledge for the People*, Toronto: OISE Press

— (1991). Dangerous knowledge: Canadian workers' education in the decades of discord, *Studies in the Education of Adults*, Vol. 23, pp. 24–40

— (1993a). Social revolutionary learning: the new social movements as learning sites, *Adult Education Quarterly*, Vol. 43, No. 3, pp. 152–64

— (1993b). Memories in the time of troubles: the liberatory moments history project. Introduction to special issue of *Convergence*, Vol. XXVI, No. 4, pp. 3–7

— (1993c). In search of the object: historiography and adult education, *Studies in Continuing Education*, Vol. 15, No. 2, pp. 133–48

Wexler, P. (1987). *Social Analysis of Education*, New York: Routledge

Wilkes, G. (1978). *A Dictionary of Australian Colloquialisms*, Sydney: Fontana/Collins

Williams, R. (1961). *The Long Revolution*, Harmondsworth: Penguin

— (1973). Base and superstructure in Marxist cultural theory, *New Left Review*, Vol. 82, pp. 3–16

— (1989). *Resources of Hope. Culture, Democracy, Socialism*, London: Verso

Willis, P. (1978). *Learning to Labour: how working-class kids get working-class jobs*, Westmead: Saxon House

Wood, E. M. (1986). *The Retreat from Class: A New 'True' Socialism*, London: Verso

— (1995). *Democracy against Capitalism: Renewing Historical Materialism*, Cambridge: Cambridge University Press

Yeatman, A. (1993). Corporate managerialism and the shift from the welfare to the competition state, *Discourse*, Vol. 13, pp. 3–9

Youngman, F. (1986). *Adult Education and Socialist Pedagogy*, London: Croom Helm

# Index